69

EXPLORING SCOTLAND WITH TOM WEIR

EXPLORING SCOTLAND
WITH TOM WEIR

Text and Photographs
by
Tom Weir

PELHAM BOOKS

PELHAM BOOKS

Published by the Penguin Group
27 Wrights Lane, London W8 5TZ, England
Viking Penguin, a division of Penguin Books USA Inc
375 Hudson Street, New York, NY 10014 USA
Penguin Books Australia Ltd, Ringwood, Victoria, Australia
Penguin Books Canada Ltd, 10 Alcorn Avenue, Suite 300, Toronto, Ontario, Canada M4V 3B2
Penguin Books (NZ) Ltd, 182–190 Wairau Road, Auckland 10, New Zealand
Penguin Books Ltd, Registered Offices: Harmondsworth, Middlesex, England

First Published 1991
1 3 5 7 9 10 8 6 4 2

Photoset in 12 on 14pt Linotron Ehrhardt
by Cambrian Typesetters, Frimley, Surrey

Printed and bound in Great Britain by
Butler & Tanner Ltd, Frome and London

A CIP catalogue record for this book is available from the British Library.

ISBN 07207 1994 1

Frontispiece: *This house below the ridge of Arcuil in Sutherlandshire is well-named 'Lone', and today is used as a bothy for adventurous walkers exploring the wilds of the Reay Forest.*

Contents

INTRODUCTION

Most days when I am at home on Loch Lomondside, where I have lived for the last 32 years, I take a walk to the top of the wee round hill our villagers call 'The Dumpling', a 463 ft. crag-and-tail commanding a mighty view of Highlands and Lowlands from its bald summit. On winter days you can be above the clouds, in spring yellow whins and bluebells scent the air, oaks and birches ring with songs of tree pipits, wood and willow warblers; the rattle of woodpecker overlaps with the drumming of snipe. In summer bracken becomes a green jungle, but colours to brilliant yellows and reds in autumn. It is a wonderfully atmospheric hill for appreciating the roll of the clouds and changes of temperature. The exercise of walking up and running down usually releases in me the desire to write – a desire which first manifested itself in my early teens when I started going to the hills 62 years ago.

It was the writings of hillman and naturalist Seton Gordon which first fired my imagination when, as a message boy in a grocer's shop, I began discovering the hills which surround Glasgow where I lived. Seton Gordon lived on the Isle of Skye, and seemed to me to lead an idyllic life, out in every season, wandering Scotland, studying wildlife, mingling with Highlanders and Islanders of all classes, taking photographs and producing book after book.

Seton Gordon had an aristocratic background. His mother was the Queen's poetess. Deeside was where he was brought up. I was a working-class lad. How could a life like his be mine? There was only one way open to me, to train myself. So I bought a simple camera, learned how to enlarge and print the photographs I took, began writing the kind of illustrated articles newspapers and magazines might take, and could have papered a house with rejection slips. Then almost magically the tide turned, and in the spring of 1939 I left the grocery job to try my hand at being a budding Seton Gordon.

It was an ill-timed period to strike out, with war in the offing, paper rationing and hostilities in which I was caught from May 1940 to January 1946. Being a serving soldier was not time wasted however. Far from it. I continued to write, was trained as a battery surveyor in the Royal Artillery, and when demobilised went into the Ordnance Survey. Working on triangulation reconnaissance all over Britain I saved enough money in four years to resign my job and set off with three Scottish Mountaineering Club friends on the very first post-war expedition which resulted in a book, *The Scottish Himalayan Expedition* by W. H. Murray, with illustrations by Douglas Scott and myself.

Following that up, I wrote a shorter version, 'High Adventure in the Himalaya' which was published in the *National Geographic Magazine* with 24 pages of colour photographs in August 1952. That was a scoop which netted us $2,500, which we used to launch another expedition to the Nepal Himalaya whose frontier, hitherto closed to foreigners, had newly opened; so we were amongst its first mountain explorers at a time when Tibetans were fleeing south from Chinese invaders across the highest passes in the world.

In 1951, between these trips, two of us had spent six weeks in arctic Norway. Douglas Scott had resigned his job at the same time as I did, so we put the '50s to good use by making expeditioning a way of life. Between foreign trips I was finding more and more joy in Scotland, climbing, skiing and writing about its wildlife and scenery. There was so much I still had to discover.

It was about this time Arthur Daw, editor of *The Scots Magazine*, phoned asking me if I could meet him in Glasgow with a view to commissioning me to write a regular monthly feature. As I had already written some longish illustrated pieces, and had found suggestions for their improvement helpful, I said I was interested.

What he invited me to do was write a 'diary' piece every month, with a good mix of subjects. 'You have a wide range of interests, but don't overplay the mountains and the wildlife. Make more of the interesting people you meet. Would you like to try it for a year?' I said I would, though I stressed that it might have to include some foreign trips. So it was agreed.

In April 1956 appeared my first regular contribution labelled by the editor 'My Month' and sub-titled 'A Strange Experience in Glencoe'. In the beginning I worried that I might not find enough to write about. In fact I had too much, because of so many happenings in Scotland: huge hydro-electricity schemes requiring reservoirs behind huge dams to submerge areas of glens where I had lodged or camped in Strathfarrar, Glen Cannich, Glen Affric, Glen Garry, Glen Mor and Glen Moriston. Waters of Glen Lyon had been harnessed to link up with Glen Lochay. My view was that these hydro-electric schemes were logical and long overdue. However I took the opposite view when the hydro-electrocution of the Glen Nevis gorge was proposed, since it was a minor scheme at a time when oil was cheap, and the gorge was without dispute the finest combination of waterfall, cliff and fragment of natural woodland in Scotland. It was reprieved after a conservation battle.

There were other issues to highlight, such as the use of toxic chemicals lowering the breeding success of golden eagles, peregrine falcons and other birds of prey at the top end of the food chain. Small birds too were disappearing as miles of hedgerows were being torn up to allow prairie farming. The destruction was aided by government grants, as was the draining of wetlands. Investors were finding that money did grow on trees because of tax advantages, hence the great blankets of North American trees springing up, while remnants of our primeval Caledonian pine forest were dying of neglect. In the deer forests where there used to be pony tracks, bulldozed roads for vehicles were proliferating.

The problems are still with us, but as more and more motor-car owners were taking to the countryside for recreation, the voices of the conservationists were getting louder and louder as an increasing number of the public realised what was happening. But the green movement is more words than deeds as yet.

The '50s and '60s produced revolutionary changes. In South Uist crofters were worried about proposals for a rocket range on their lands for firing missiles into the Atlantic, to be tracked from remote St Kilda where a radar and military base was to be set up. I had been to St Kilda in the mid-1950s when a dozen of us hired a fishing boat from Scalpay in Harris, and camped for a fortnight on Hirta, seeing the remote settlement as it had been when the islanders evacuated it 25 years before, at their own request. Little could I have guessed then that my next arrival in Village Bay would be from the open mouth of a military landing barge in April 1957, bringing in equipment for the men of Operation Hardrock who were building a base and beachhead for a future garrison that would man a radar tracking station when it was built on top of the hill.

My job was to take photographs that would show what life was like for the men then living in a tented camp, and working right round the clock. I

9

was also there to enjoy myself in the good company of two fine naturalists, Kenneth Williamson and Dr W. J. Eggeling, who were acting as watchdogs for the National Trust for Scotland and the Nature Conservancy to ensure that the least possible damage to wildlife interests was done during building operations. They were also taking the chance to do what had never been done before at this period of peak bird migration between Scotland and Iceland – trap and ring birds – finding much that had never been recorded before on St Kilda.

Also by a neat coincidence, the Ordnance Survey team with whom I used to work were on the island tying its highest point into the triangulation network for the first time in history. It took them a month to complete their observations.

Because I was on the move so much I learned to write wherever I happened to be, in camp, bothy, boat or train. In 1970 I had the new experience of writing from a hospital bed after a rock-climbing fall which squashed my spine, cracked my hip and damaged my rib cage. Luckily I covered this out-of-action period by writing a portrait of the Isle of Rum, which had an unexpected historical reward.

Rum of the Inner Hebrides was entirely cleared of its Gaelic-speaking people by McLean of Coll who assisted their emigration and replaced them with 8,000 sheep. But finding the island was undermanned, he brought over a dozen families from Skye. Examining a tombstone erected by Murdo Matheson I wondered if he was one of these incomers. The stone tells of five of his children who died in two days, of diphtheria, in 1877.

After my 'Portrait of Rum' had appeared in *The Scots Magazine*, came a letter from Miss Helen Matheson of Otago in New Zealand giving me the sequel to these tragic deaths.

'Following the diphtheria epidemic Murdo Matheson and his wife sailed here with their five remaining children to try and build a new life. One died shortly after arriving in Otago. In March 1876 Murdo obtained a job as shepherd on Copperbrook Station, at an annual wage of £65, among 80,000 merino sheep.

'Murdo was sent to a hirsel known as Bald Hill, and 20 years later the owner of this section was Murdo's son Dougald, and the farm had been renamed Attadale, after Attadale on Loch Carron in Wester Ross, the seat of the clan Matheson. Dougald married in 1897 and had three sons and a daughter. One of these sons is my father.'

Miss Helen Matheson had been to the Isle of Rum and described her visit thus:

> 'I shall never forget that day, August 24th, 1966. It was a perfect summer's day. It seemed an achievement to find the gravestone. But sad to think that one part of the family is buried on the Island of Rum and the remainder in the little country churchyard of Middlemarch in Central Otago, New Zealand.
>
> 'It was so interesting to note that the countryside where they chose to live was similar to Rum, outcrops of volcanic rock, mountains, peatbogs and tussock grass.'

That is just one sample of the fascinating contacts I've made through 'My Month', so that now when I write I know I am speaking to readers all over the world, as well as to those in Britain who can see beyond the triviality of tartan and haggis. The country you will explore with me is the real Scotland.

ACROSS SCOTLAND:
GLEN AFFRIC TO KINTAIL

IN FRONT OF ME, as I write, is a letter in beautiful script from Duncan MacLennan of Glen Affric Lodge,* an isolated dwelling midway between the North Sea at Beauly and the Atlantic seaboard at Loch Duich. Stretching from sea to sea, this is one of the truly great cross-country routes, a challenging push for a cyclist, since some hard stuff on bog and rock has to be walked. Hikers who get a lift to where the public road stops short of the Lodge have the best of it, especially if they can be met on the west side at Morvich as happened to me the first time I made the big crossing.

Duncan's letter begins: 'I enjoyed seeing you very much yesterday and I hope you had a good walk through the glen. The weather looked gloomy in the west, but I hope the visibility wasn't too bad. I would dearly have loved to be along with you to discuss the history of the glen. In my 40 years here I've seen many changes.'

The last time I had talked to Duncan was seven years ago in winter blizzard conditions which made a Canadian Rockies scene of snow-laden Caledonian pines, glittering loch and flawless white peaks after the storm had passed. With me that day was Forestry Commission District Officer Finlay Macrae, who had just been awarded a statuette of a phoenix rising from the ashes, for his sustained management of the Caledonian pines which are the major glory of this glen. He was with me again on this trip, together with a BBC producer, Suzanne Gibbs, and her sound recordist, who was to tape snatches of our conversation on the walk.

Finlay is retired from the Commission now. A Gaelic speaker from the Isle of Skye, he had begun as an ordinary forestry hand in Glen Brittle, gone on to Aberdeen University, and graduated under Professor H. M.

* Duncan MacLennan in retirement now lives in Cannich Village.

Finlay Macrae (left) and Duncan MacLennan, two men who know Glen Affric intimately, and whose knowledge added greatly to the walk between the North Sea and the Atlantic.

Steven, who inspired Finlay with his advocacy for the regeneration of the Caledonian pine. Professor Steven was seeing Sitka spruces and other fast-growing alien species blanketing hillsides within protecting fences, while our priceless Caledonian woods in 35 locations were being allowed to die.

Finlay had driven from Flodigarry in Skye to meet us in Cannich, and when he talked about the wild weather I knew what he meant, for fierce squalls had buffeted me, rocking the car on the drive up Loch Linnhe. We counted ourselves lucky to waken to fitful sunshine, and no more than a snell breeze next morning.

The colours, dulling one moment and glowing the next, were almost beyond description: scarlet rowans, golden birches, pink bark of bottle-green pines, smoke-yellow larches. In a short distance we were at Loch Benavean and looking down on the small concrete dam which holds it in. Finlay had things worth pointing out. 'Look below you at the density of birches with pines pushing through. These are growing on the spoil heaps taken from the tunnels and dumped here during the building of the hydro-electric scheme. This new Glen Affric road is higher than the old one, but look at it now – fringed everywhere with growing pine and birch. They'll have to be cut in places or the fine views of the loch will be lost.'

He also pointed out the contrasts that fencing has produced: thriving young Caledonian pines within their boundaries, but only the old trees outside and no regeneration because the deer graze them down. Round the 4,300 acres of Caledonian pinewood reserve stretch 200 miles of deer fencing.

Not until you are well up the glen do you see the peaks. The classic view is where you look down on the short river that flows out of Loch Affric with the rocky horn of Sgurr na Lapaich rising abruptly beyond. Edged by scattered pines is Duncan's cottage and he was at the door to welcome us.

In no time we were inside, the kettle was on the boil, and cups of coffee were in our hands. He apologised for his wife not being there because, this being the deer-stalking season, she was attending guests at the Lodge close by. The weather had been good, so they were well on the way to getting their quota of stags. We had seen the tactful notices at the end of the public road: 'Deer stalking in progress, 1st August to 15th October. Please keep off the hills.'

'It's only deer on the hills now. We no longer have any sheep, so one of my sons is away and lives at Cannich.' Duncan expanded on this point in his letter. 'I had an eagle's nest on a rock in sight of the house, and the year after the sheep went, the eagles disappeared. I often saw them perched on a sheep carcase during the winter. We killed 40 foxes a year when we had the sheep, and always saw foxes on the hill during the stalking. We have only two dens now against eight or nine before. Where there is a big stock of sheep there is always a carcase about. The last two winters there were no deer carcases and the hoodie crow was feeding on the blocks we put out for the deer, a sign that carrion was scarce.'

It would have been grand to sit longer over that coffee and cake, but with 18 miles before us we were going to need all the daylight hours. Finlay remarked on a tree as we passed the Lodge, 'That Caledonian pine was drawn by Landseer, and it's still recognisable today by its branches which are unchanged since Victorian times.'

Redwings were flighting on the rowans, and crossbills sounding up in the trees as we walked on under the highest summits north-west of the Great Glen. High ridges connect Carn Eighe and Mam Soul, both over 3,800 ft., and burns in spate poured down side glens, one with an impressive waterfall. Finlay gave me its Gaelic name, Sputan Ban, meaning white spout, a perfect description.

Rickles of stones tell of summer shielings by the green pastures on each side of the river. Duncan thinks the stones for one, named Old Colan, must have been sledged in by ponies. This ruin, with its neatly-rounded ends, is supposed to have been lived in by a bard: one severe winter he lost all his black cattle, and before he left the glen he wrote a sad song about it.

As a lunching spot we had chosen what was the last occupied house in the loneliest stretch of the glen, Alltbeithe, now a youth hostel. We could see it about two miles ahead, but because of the soft ground demanding detours, it took a long time to reach. Duncan's letter mentioned something very interesting about this bit. 'When I came to Affric you could take a horse and cart to Alltbeithe no bother at all. Now the pathway is in the middle of the river in places. I took the beds into Alltbeithe, getting them there by horse and cart. It would be difficult to take a pack-horse nowadays in wet weather.'

Before we reached Alltbeithe, we were getting rain from the lowering clouds, so it was good to find the door unlatched and sit down at the table, pour out tea from the flasks and see what was in our sandwich packets. It was while we were munching that the sole occupants arrived, a young man from Dundee and his springer spaniel. I had been telling of my pre-war visit here in the 1930s when it was home to a large family of Hendersons who had their own resident school teacher, and everybody was glad to stop work and hear news from outside. In fact I had come from Benula in Glen Cannich where I'd been camping near the house of Duncan MacLennan's brother, and had risen at dawn to set out for Loch Duichside at 4 p.m. where I had a rendezvous with a climbing pal.

I certainly don't remember anything so boggy and unpleasant as the next bit of the path across a no-man's-land of sodden peat. I'm sure I would have remembered it if it had been as bad the last time I was here. It fairly slowed up the BBC team, but once over the pass, things improved as we reached the place marked Camban on the map. It was a ruin, until restored as a memorial bothy commemorating two young climbers, Tranter and Park. Philip Tranter, who used to write for *The Scots Magazine*, was killed in a car crash; Park died in a rock-climbing accident in Sutherland.

'Camban must have been a remote abode in winter,' wrote Duncan MacLennan in his letter. 'It was a resting place for the droves and I'm sure many a good story was told there and many a good dram tossed over. When the drove left there for Cluanie, they skirted round the east shoulder of Ciste Dhubh. The mark on the hillside can be seen quite clearly from the opposite side of the glen. The last occupant, Paterson by name, left at the beginning of the century.'

15

End of the walk was Loch Duich below the Five Sisters of Kintail, seen left, but the approach was from behind the peaks.

There are some tiring ups and downs after Camban, traversing into an ever wilder scene as the ground falls away to Glen Lichd. We were the closest we had been yet to roaring stags, and stopped to watch a black-maned giant, antlers back and head up as he sent out his deep-throated bellowing challenge to warn potential rivals off his 47 hinds. This is a threat display to intimidate lesser animals, and is usually effective until a challenger answers bellow with bellow. If one doesn't give way to the other, there is a fight for possession of the harem. A fast-flying eagle passed across our line of sight as we watched the neurotic antics of the stags around us.

What was now a bit worrying was the slower speed of our companions, and Finlay came up with the idea that I should go ahead and get to our rendezvous point and arrange for a vehicle to come up Glen Lichd. From the heights to the glen is quite a sudden drop, as the path becomes a rock staircase through impressive waterfalls and smooth slabs. Lichd comes from the Gaelic 'Leac', meaning slabs, so Glen Lichd is well named.

The fading daylight made me force the pace, though I would have loved to linger and enjoy the narrow throat of gorge walls where waters roared and stags bellowed. Mist swirled round the rock teeth, revealing them as silhouettes an immense height among the clouds.

Down on the glen bottom, then across two swollen burns, a climb up to the rough track and I could make good speed, pushing as hard as I could to beat the darkness. I was enjoying being alone, too, in a world that seemed empty and rather menacing. Then suddenly I was blinded by a headlight, and as I stood aside a Land-Rover pulled up and out hopped the manager of Cannich Hotel.

His own vehicle was only 100 yards from our rendezvous point. As darkness fell and we had not shown up, he had alerted the mountain rescue, and a local deerstalker had abandoned everything to drive up the glen to investigate.

They were greatly relieved to hear how things were, and the weary pair were delighted to be lifted down the final stretch. Finlay, of course, had been a tower of strength, and once the wet clothes were off, and with a dram inside us, it was a merry party who arrived back at Cannich after the long drive by Glen Shiel and Glen Moriston to Drumnadrochit and Glen Urquhart. Waiting for us, too, was a fine meal despite the time being 10 p.m. It would be near midnight when Finlay set off back to Dingwall where he lives when he is not in Skye.

The morning saw me back up the glen in my own car to let the BBC folk pick up their vehicle from where they had left it the previous day.

In Glen Affric I had seen only redwings, but on the drive back down the Great Glen I saw my first fieldfares of the winter, and on Ben Nevis and the Glencoe hills there was a good powder of new snow. Ben Lomond also had quite a substantial cap, which pleased me greatly for I was due to appear in a 'Highway' television programme with Harry Secombe and wanted Loch Lomondside to be looking its best.

It did, too, and wise-cracking Harry was great fun as he sang 'By Yon Bonnie Banks' on the Luss shore and kept us all in good humour, undaunted by the cold north wind. He generated his own warmth.

30 YEARS OF OSPREYS

IT WAS A delightful surprise to receive a phone call from the RSPB camp at Loch Garten to tell me that three young ospreys in the nest were well-fledged and ready for ringing. Then came an invitation: would I be prepared to travel up with Pat Sandeman and celebrate 30 years of the greatest success story of modern conservation?

'We want to put on a show in the Osprey Suite of the Aviemore Centre telling the tale from the beginning, and that's the bit that involves you and Pat, for you were among the first in on it. Since those early days when the ospreys came to Loch Garten, 600 young birds have flown from Scottish eyries, 400 of them with numbered rings on their legs. We've something very worthwhile to celebrate.'

I said we would certainly be there, and my wife, too. So it was with happy anticipation we collected Pat and drove up the A9 in cheerful sunshine, enjoying the moving cloudscape above Dunkeld, and the grey heights of Atholl to heathery Drumochter and over that high pass to enter the different country of broad Badenoch and Strathspey.

The new line of the A9 fairly shows off the setting of the snow-dappled Cairngorms distinctively cut by the pinkish notch of the Lairig Ghru over foothills of Caledonian pines spreading across from Rothiemurchus to Glen Feshie.

In Aviemore it was not only good to meet up with other speakers, but to see so many of the public filling the seats.

My remit was to talk with slides for 20 minutes, setting the Cairngorm scene, showing the primeval forest, the lochs where the ospreys used to breed, Loch Morlich, Loch an Eilean, and the Cairngorm plateau, a true fragment of the Arctic in Scotland, carved with corries where semi-permanent snows lie in the shadow of great horseshoe cliffs. Here, in the great tract of unpopulated country between the Dee and the Spey, spanned only by long distance paths, is Scotland's greatest wildlife wilderness. Roy Dennis in his excellent low-cost book *Birds of Badenoch and Strathspey* lists 219 species here, including the osprey.

That was the inspiring story the audience had come to hear. Last century, egg collectors and sportsmen had robbed or gunned down the last Speyside ospreys at Loch an Eilean and Loch Morlich. Then, quite suddenly, in 1954 they were back in one of their old haunts, building an eyrie and rearing two young birds.

Even the RSPB didn't hear of it until a year later when the news was made public.

Here was a problem. Egg collectors would converge on Speyside. If ospreys were going to succeed in recolonising old haunts they would have to be watched and guarded. So between 1956 and 1958, the RSPB had watchers in Strathspey looking out for ospreys returning from West Africa where they winter.

In this big scale country of forest, river and hills, the task was patience-testing, especially since another eyrie had been discovered in the Loch Garten woods. George Waterston, who was master-minding the operation, saw his faith pay off. In May 1958, I had a phone call from him with the code-word that meant ospreys were nesting, and the map reference of where I would find him.

When he said my help was urgently needed, he meant it. There were only five for a round-the-clock vigil on the eyrie, and he needed six. Within hours I was there and, at four o'clock in the morning, relieving George on night watch.

I had been carefully briefed. In the hide was a stout cord. At the other end of it a short distance off would be George, having a well-earned snooze, with a loop of cord on his wrist. A tug from me would mean an alarm and he would come running. Through the binoculars clamped on their tripod, we viewed the upper part of the pine, surmounted by a huge nest above whose rim was the head of the brooding bird.

George had told me I would get my first view of a flying osprey at dawn when the male came to the nest. The dawn chorus of woodland birds had begun, and a warm glow was spreading over the eastern sky when the osprey appeared with powerful strokes of broad wings, angled like those of a gull until it threw them back, long legs down and claws bunched to land on the eyrie.

I enjoyed these watches, seeing the male bringing fish to the female, getting to know their squeals and whistles, at the same time relishing

19

sightings of crossbills, capercaillie, crested tits, roe deer and red squirrels.

It was a quiet time for me, but not for Philip Brown a fortnight after I left. It was the third week of incubation and the Director of the RSPB was looking forward to the dawn, when, in the near darkness, he made out the movement of a climber on the tree. He tugged the alarm cord, yelled, ran, promptly fell on his face, got up, was joined by Bert Axell, and together they tore on over the rough ground. They were too late. On the grass was the white blob of a broken osprey egg, and later they found another.

That is the point where I ended my tale. Frank Hamilton took over, telling of the wave of public indignation which followed the disclosure of the story in the Press. Yet the mean action was to have the reverse effect intended by the egg thief. Instead of doing harm to the RSPB, it did them good in more ways than one. First, because the ospreys built a new nest in a better position for observation and defence against intrusion. Second, because the public became intensely interested in the ospreys.

All looked set for success in 1959 until part of the forest went on fire and flames swept in the direction of the nest.

Frank Hamilton, now Director of the RSPB in Scotland, was a new recruit then, and he told his audience of the fight to halt the raging fire before it got to the birds. Then came a miracle. Just when the fighters were failing through fatigue, the wind shifted to the opposite direction.

It was after this scare that George Waterston came up with the suggestion that Director Philip Brown regarded as quite crazy. Why not invite the public to visit the hide, provide big high-powered binoculars and encourage them to make a donation to the funds or join the Society? It was tried, and in seven weeks 14,000 people came, some ornithologists certainly, but mostly ordinary tourists.

Tourists have been the life-blood of 'Operation Osprey' ever since. No fewer than 1⅓ million have visited the site to date, their financial contributions through donations and membership fees transforming the RSPB, previously bedevilled

George Waterston, Royal Society for the Protection of Birds' Scottish Director, who master-minded the return of the osprey to Loch Garten.

The observer's view from the forward hide as the osprey flies in with a fish for the young perched on the rim of the nest on top of the Caledonian pine tree.

by lack of funds, into a body powerful enough to purchase threatened habitats all over Britain and make them into wardened bird reserves. It focused attention on what the word 'conservation' means.

Roy Dennis, Highland Officer of the RSPB, and cameraman Chris Mylne spoke next; Roy, with slides, taking us graphically through the decades, updating what has been discovered about ospreys, and revealing their current healthy status in terms of breeding population.

In 1985, it looked as if the good luck at Loch Garten had run out when the male osprey damaged a wing and had to be put into care. The female abandoned the eggs and they were placed in an incubator. The one healthy young bird that survived was fostered by another osprey with chicks of a similar age, which was some consolation.

Two years ago the terrible discovery was made that vandals had been at work sawing through a vital section of the osprey tree. But the RSPB got working in time, strengthening the tree and building a brand new artificial eyrie which the returning ospreys used. Alas, the eggs failed.

Would the birds succeed in 1987? The ospreys mated, eggs were laid, but broken by the birds. So fingers were crossed this year with the happy result of three young birds raised to flying stage. It made a grand total of 54 ospreys from Loch Garten in 30 years, a higher than normal productivity.*

Ringing so many young before they left the nest has resulted in 35 recoveries. The farthest north was between Greenland and Iceland, from a fishing boat; the farthest south, West Africa. Other records of ringed Scottish birds have come from all over Europe on migration between here and their winter quarters in West Africa. Ospreys, said Roy, used to be

* Despite failure of Loch Garten ospreys to rear young to final success, osprey numbers in 1990 are the highest yet: 62 pairs attempted, 87 young flew from eyries and eight nests were robbed by egg thieves.

shot in hundreds in Europe, but now they suffer very little, largely because the whole world knows about the Loch Garten pairs through the power of television.

What I was looking forward to after the interval were clips from the film that the famous cameraman Hugh Miles was making at Loch Garten on the life of the osprey. He is the man who filmed 'The Flight of the Condor', 'Track of the Wild Otter' and 'Kingdom of the Ice Bear'.

Small, strong, bearded and humorous, he told us some of his secrets, such as putting trout in a cage so he could film the birds diving against the composition he wanted, then throwing out food pellets to bring the fish to the surface when the osprey was in the vicinity.

Nor was it just the shot of any dive he was after. It had to be when the sun was against him, so that the splash would glitter like reflected crystal against the dark background of the hills. The osprey's glide, and downward tilt, when legs and claws go out like the arms of a diving human, have never been better portrayed, nor has the moment when, with wings beating the surface water, it rises with a wriggling fish in one talon.

Once clear of the water and making height, there is another special moment when the osprey shakes its head dry like a dog. Hugh got it in full close-up, but not to his satisfaction. It didn't shake its head against the background he wanted, but he'll keep trying until he captures it.

Two other brilliant shots stick in my mind. An osprey beating in silhouette against a splendid sunrise, pitching down on top of a pine; but this time the colours are on every feather, orange, red, cream, brown, and so close you feel you could touch them. The other shows the osprey picking up a long, thick double branch you would judge too heavy for any bird. It uses its flying momentum to lift it clear without landing. It is no surprise that the osprey builds the biggest nest of any predator.

It was raining and misty as we left that marvellous presentation and headed for Roy Dennis's home at Inchdryne in the Abernethy Forest, where in the cheerful living-room we chatted with Roy and his wife Marina before going to bed. In the morning we woke to find ourselves in a cheerful green oasis which has been the base for the osprey watchers from the beginning.

The crofthouse was a new one, and after breakfast we crossed to the whitewashed original, where lives Marina's aunt, Miss Isabel MacDonald, famed amongst all osprey watchers for her hospitality. As I sat down she held up *The Scots Magazine* saying, 'I still follow you every month.' Although crippled now with arthritis, her hearing is good and her eyes bright. As well as running the croft, she made her home a happy place for orphan children, acting as foster mother to countless of them over the years.

Little did Roy know when he joined the staff of the RSPB and took over the management of 'Operation Osprey' in 1960 that three years later he would meet his future wife and marry her the same year. Roy was 23 and Marina 20, and together they took over the wardenship of the Fair Isle Bird Observatory, adding in the next seven years another three to the population of that remote spot between Orkney and Shetland, first a girl and then two boys.

Roy reminisced with Marina over their arrival in their new home, 'The first thing that was said to us as old Jackie Wilson helped us off with our gear was, "I hope you can dance." It was on Fair Isle we really learned about the world. It's an experience we wouldn't have missed. My later job of Highland Officer to the RSPB with a base in the Black Isle also couldn't have been timed better.

'Now we're crofters, growing oats, hay and turnips to feed our sheep and cattle. We have 40 acres with rough grazing, and a fifth share of 1,000 acres of common grazing. It's very satisfying after a day in the office to come home, put a couple of hay bales on my shoulder and have the cows come to meet me for their winter feed. I like to stand there and just listen to them munching; it gives me a real feeling of belonging.'

The family is now grown up. Rona is a geographer; Gavin an accountant; and Roddy at university. Marina finds herself driving about 30,000 miles a year as a producer for Radio Highland. She says, however, she is a crofter at heart, born and brought up at Roy Bridge and descended from a famous cattle reiver, Coll of the Cows. It's good to know that the croft is now in such loving hands.

Those ospreys certainly started something when they flew in to Loch Garten.

KILLIECRANKIE AND THE WHISKY TRAIL TO DEESIDE

MY OLD FRIEND Pat Sandeman had a suggestion for an outing: 'Let's take a look at the new stretch of the A9 at Killiecrankie. After we've seen that we'll go back down the old road to the Tenandry. Have you been there?'

I hadn't, but I liked the idea.

The new fast A9 from Stirling has certainly taken the aggro out of driving north, if you are in a hurry. One by one the villages have been by-passed, and now, after 14 years' work, the 'impossible' steeps of Killiecrankie are tamed by a mighty piece of civil engineering involving 640 yards of viaduct, 300 yards of it dual carriageway. To build the road on concrete stilts required four temporary haul roads in parallel, and resident geologists to advise on the stability of the gullied hillside. One dumper driver was killed when his vehicle left a haul road and turned over and over down into the gorge.

So we didn't take the new road for granted as we spun over it, enjoying the unique views through the windscreen. Leaving this engineering marvel just over its crest by the link road to Blair Atholl, we were soon turning down the old Pass of Killiecrankie road, then taking the first right over the railway and the river before winding up a narrow climbing road to Balrobie farm, our destination.

Parking the car, we knocked at the door, but the Warden was out. I say Warden for this is Royal Society for the Protection of Birds ground, and he looks after it. I didn't even know there was such a place, or that I was in for a great treat, for the farm is below an escarpment of crags hung with birches and crowned with heather, with access paths open to the public. In a box just opposite the car park was a leaflet, with an explanatory map showing the three-hour circuit round Craig Fonvuick, 1,345 ft.

This walk is a little gem. You start up the road to a gate opposite another farm and then follow yellow markers up a zig-zagging climbing path with striking views opening out to the Pass of Killiecrankie and the big curve of the new engineering wonders carved from the hillsides, and remarkably unobtrusive they look in this large scale countryside of river and mountain.

The sky had been overcast as we climbed, then, just before we reached the heather, shafts of sun filtered through, putting a red sheen on the heather, making the greenery more emerald and the grey rocks of Beinn a'Ghlo brighter.

Pat pointed out the site of the Battle of Killiecrankie on the steep open slope west of Glen Girnaig. 'That's where the Highland army swept down, barefooted, and overwhelmed Mackay's troops with such speed that the fight was all over in a few minutes.

'The troops of William and Mary hadn't even time to draw their bayonets against the Jacobites. It's said that Bonnie Dundee didn't attack in the pass because he was such a gentleman; he didn't want to take them at a disadvantage, but make it a fair fight. He was one of the few casualties, stopping a bullet and dying on the field. Mackay was able to push on and at Inverlochy on Loch Linnhe built a fortification which he called Fort William.'

At the limit of the trees we came into a delightful bowl, with the ruins of an old township under a cirque of field dyke, and traces of cultivation rigs still showing on ground which was a mixture of bog cotton and richly-coloured heather. A heavy shower was developing, so we took advantage of the shelter to eat our pieces, pondering on the lifestyle of the Gaelic-speaking folk who lived here, growing what they could and tending cattle. Here at 1,000 ft. above sea-level the season would be short, for winter comes early and springs are late in Atholl.

On top of the hill we were trying to identify the very first road to Inverness built by General Wade, and decided we'd go looking for it as we struck south-west, leaving the honey-scented heather for regenerating larch and birch, then to a green flush of watery ground bright with flowers. There was grass of Parnassus, sweet-scented orchis, yellow mountain saxifrage and a virtual meadow of bog cotton, harebells and devil's bit. Long may this well-cared-for Reserve survive, for such variety is getting rare.

We drove north for Calvine, parking on the old A9 where Gleann a' Chrombaidh flows into the deep cut of the River Garry. What we had to do now was walk the short distance to the busy new A9, nip smartly across it, then take to the woods and follow up the waterfalls of the Chrombaidh to discover, a few hundred feet above us, what we were looking for, Wade's bridge, known locally as Drochaid na h-Unneige, the Window Bridge.

Appearing to grow out of the rocks, its neat single arch looked invulnerable to time though it must date back to about 1728, since it was about then that Wade's squads of 300 to 600 men were tackling the boulders and bogs of the Drumochter Pass for 6d a day more than a normal soldier's pay. The military road they were building to Inverness was for marching soldiers and pack-carrying horses. Not until the Tay was bridged by Telford at Dunkeld did the first stagecoach operate from Inverness. It set out from the Highland capital at 5 a.m., reaching Perth at 3 p.m. after 10 hours of exciting driving. The historic year of this big breakthrough in communications was 1809.

Telford's improvements dated from 1803, and before then getting to Inverness was an adventure. In the space of 20 years, Telford and his men had '. . . succeeded in effecting a change in the state of the Highlands unparalleled in the same space of time in the history of any country'. As late as 1973, however, the A9 was more akin to the age of Telford than to the 20th century age of motorways. In that year, John Webster, garage owner at Calvine, told me he was hauling 300-400 wrecked vehicles annually off the A9, and that was only on his stretch of the death-trap road.

Despite land-use changes made over the years, there was no problem following the Wade track. Walking for a mile eastward, Pat pointed out to me how it kept a high line to the West Lodge of Blair Castle and Old Blair kirkyard where Bonnie Dundee's bones once lay.* Slanting northward from the bridge, edging a plantation, it keeps its contour and crosses another burn before being absorbed in the present A9 about a mile on.

Compare the times from Perth to Inverness in a car against stagecoach performances in Telford's day – roughly an hour and a half against 10 hours.

Given time, however, I still prefer the byways to rushing on, and with the faster roads the quiet ways where you can stop and look around have become even quieter. How nice it was, recently, to follow down the Spey from Grantown and enjoy its windings by yellow barley fields and pastures of grazing cattle to its broad stretch at Aberlour where fishermen

* The remains of Bonnie Dundee were removed, but the memorial plaque on the vault commemorates him. There is a tradition that, mortally wounded in the battle, he was carried to the Inn at Old Blair where he died – just a step from the kirk.

Drochaid na h-Unneige – the Window Bridge – built by General Wade. It dates back to about 1728 when his squads of 300 to 600 men were tackling the boulders and bogs to make a military road to Inverness.

in waders stood out as far as they dared, casting for salmon in the dark flowing water.

Most of the way down I had been seeing 'Whisky Trail' signs for I had entered the golden triangle where whisky-making was a cottage industry when there was corn enough to produce it, and before restrictions on folk's freedom to do so. Licences to produce whisky became necessary in the very year the Kilmarnock Edition of the poetry of Robert Burns was published, exactly 200 years ago, in 1786, when Strathisla distillery in Keith was set up and became the first on the Scottish mainland to hold a licence.

Of course, it opened the door for the illegal trade, whose whisky was said to be a lot better than the legal stuff in those early days. It has been said that most of the distilleries in the golden triangle today stand on the sites of former illegal distilleries, and use the same excellent water and peat.

I called at Strathisla distillery in Keith, and saw why it was originally called the Milton, for a mill wheel was still turning merrily. The River Isla was its source of power when two local men set it up. Today, of course, the wheel is just an ornament, set below pagoda spires of the kiln and an old-world architectural exterior which belies the distillery's modernity inside. I was told that there is evidence that whisky may have been distilled on this same site 780 years ago.

St Maelrubha, he of Loch Maree and Applecross fame, second only to St Columba in importance, set up a cell here in Keith about the year 700, and his holy well by the old kirkyard is said to have been used to make the mystical water of life. Keith today is the second largest town in Banffshire, and despite its population of over 4,000, it is very much a quiet country town where you look out on heather hills.

To be truthful, the externals of the distillery interested me more than the internals, since one modern whisky manufacturing plant tends to be like another. What was new to me was the final process of the whisky barrels from the bond being tapped open after 12 years' maturing, a sample being taken out and sniffed for quality, emptied back if approved, then the cask rotated to let the whisky run out into a lade to disappear out of sight into holding tanks. What I saw was a single malt Strathisla, disappearing. If it had been a blend, the barrels would have been of different kinds, coming together in storage with flavour according to the recipe.

I also heard about what they call the Angels' Share, the whisky that evaporates into the atmosphere during years of storage. True or false, I

The Old Bridge of Dee as the first of the sun lit the heather and brought lustre to the Caledonian pines.

was told that more whisky disappears through the wood in Scottish bonds than is sold, which means that the 'angels' get more than the Excise, despite their levy of nearly £6 a bottle, and Value Added Tax.

It was evening when I drove off for Dufftown and the Glen Livet road to Tomintoul, but such were the exciting changes of light in a world of stormclouds and shafts of sun that I just had to keep going, stopping only to look at a short-eared owl wavering over the red heather and to cast a look up to the stormy Ladder Hills.

I passed through Ballater at dusk, then drove on to Braemar and over the Devil's Elbow to knock on the door of my friend Iain who lives near Bridge of Cally. I was telling him how brilliant the heather was up on Deeside and he said, 'Margaret and I were talking only this afternoon about going up to take a look at it'.

And that's where we went, arriving at the Old Bridge of Dee as the first of the sun lit the heather and brought lustre to the Caledonian pines. Lochnagar was sombre under shadow as we crossed to Invercauld ground for the Slugain path which reaches into Glen Quoich and gives access to Beinn a' Bhuird and Ben Avon.

We were a trio until, hearing crossbills, birds which Margaret had

29

never seen, the pair of us climbed up to follow the sounds among pines and spruces for views of the red cock birds, green hens and brownish young. Their food is seeds, which they prise out from the leathery cones with their crossed pliers of bills. We had good views of them and saw a capercaillie into the bargain, but there was no sign of Iain when we went back down.

'That's just like him,' said Margaret. 'Impatient!'

Assuming he had gone on to our pre-determined destination, we were wondering, after an hour, why he wasn't in sight on the brilliant heather sweeping up to the rock slabs and warted tops of Beinn a' Bhuird.

'He's carrying the rucksack with the lunch, so he'll wait for us,' I said confidently.

In fact, Iain had assumed, when we drifted up the hill to look at the crossbills, that we had decided to make for the Loch Builg path, and he was a bit puzzled as mile followed mile and we were never even in sight.

He had been waiting at the car for an hour when we got back to it – which pleased us greatly for he never wears a watch and tends to forget all about time.

'Yes, he lives in a wee world of his own,' said Margaret.

So it was a late lunch we had, but all the more enjoyable for that.

THE GOOD LIFE

I HAVE TO THANK that assiduous editor and reviser of *Munro's Tables*, J. C. Donaldson of Braemar, for putting me in touch with 'Nell Bynack' when I put the question to him: 'Who in this neighbourhood would be the best person to talk to about life in the remote glens before and after the First World War?'

It would have to be somebody whose mind was sharp and who wouldn't be daunted by television cameras, but remain his or her natural couthie self – a tall order, but I knew as soon as I began talking with Nell that I had found the person I was looking for.

Bright-eyed, she listened to my preamble and reacted instantly: 'Well, don't expect me to put on anything fancy. I'll talk the way I've always done and you can take it or leave it.' I can only paraphrase her rich Aberdeenshire tongue which delighted us all with its crispness as well as the good sense of its content.

The real name of this spry 81-year-old is Miss Nell Macdonald. Bynack is the name of a lonely ruin deep in the hills between upper Glen Tilt and the Chest of Dee where she was brought up with three brothers and sisters when it was a snug house. Nell Bynack derives from the custom of naming a person from the house associated with them, and Nell has nothing but happy family memories of Bynack and the first 12 years of this century she spent there.

'Lonely? We never gave it a thought, there was so much to do and see. It was an open green place among trees, and we had a horse and cart for getting to Braemar. Sometimes we would walk the path and visit the two keepers at Fealar Lodge, at 1,750 ft. the highest in the Highlands they say. We had a good croft to work, with a cow and a calf for milk. We grew potatoes and other vegetables. We'd fruit bushes, too. We cut hay in two parks to feed the deer in winter. No, we didn't want for anything.

Miss Nell Macdonald, otherwise known as Nell Bynack of the Derry, from the two remote houses where she was brought up. 'Lonely? I never gave it a thought.'

'We loved it when the tinkers came to the door on their way from Glen Tilt to Deeside for farmwork – whole families of them. They came one at a time so that they would all get something. I remember a wee kitten one of them carried in a basket, and us looking at some of the things they held out for sale, pins and needles, thread and things like that.

'You didn't see many strangers in the hills in those days, just odd ones, usually professional people, from the Cairngorm Club or Scottish Mountaineering Club, looking for a bed for the night. They stayed in the house as guests, and I think they paid for their lodging. There was none of this bothying. Seton Gordon used to come about. I have a photograph of him with my father and I've got some of his books. He was the best writer of them all. Nobody else can touch him.'

Nell's gamekeeping family was the last to live permanently at the Bynack, and the next move was to a spot she found much grimmer, Luibeg, which was her home from 1912 to 1925. 'Yes, and I then became known to some folk as Nell Bynack of the Derry. It seemed an awful dark place, heather and rocks, after the greenness of the Bynack. You're 1,400 ft. up and it's the nearest house to Ben Macdhui, the second highest peak in Scotland. It gets an awful lot of snow and wind. I've always loved the hills, though, especially Ben Macdhui.

32

'I've been on the top 22 times, you know. I've seen the view from the summit when it was at its absolute clearest and you could see everything, but I've been up in the mist, too, and then you've got to be very careful. I got a bit wandered once, and had no idea where I was until I found the Sapper's Bothy. I waited and got a glimpse of Loch Etchachan, then I knew exactly where to go. It's easy to go very far wrong on the plateau when the mist is down. It's the ones who don't realise this who get into trouble. There's plenty of room to get really lost.'

She told me how it came about that she had gone up the 4,296 ft. summit so often. 'With guests from the Fife Arms Hotel at Braemar. A party would want to climb Macdhui and they would send word to me asking if I would take them up. I didn't consider myself a guide. I didn't make a charge, but I always had an enjoyable day, and I was never out of pocket for it. We always went up the Sron Riach for the lovely view you get as you go up the ridge. Then you come to the rocks with the wee Lochan Uaine in the floor of the corrie below you, and Derry Cairngorm on one side and the Devil's Point and Cairn Toul on the other.'

In the days Nell was talking about, Mar Estate stalked the high ground to Cairn Toul and maintained a summer watcher at Corrour to ensure that walkers on the Lairig Ghru kept to the path and didn't spoil the sport of deer-stalking parties who had tramped a very long way for it. Nell reminisced: 'There was no selling of venison in those days. It was given away. Critics may talk of the low wages of long ago, but I think those old times were actually better for estate workers' families than they are now when it's all money, money, money.'

I asked Robbie Mitchell, manager of Mar Lodge Estate, how the vastly increased foot traffic in his part of the Cairngorms affected deer-stalking success. 'It restricts us a bit, but we manage quite well on the whole. We accept that there will be some disturbance. It wouldn't be wise to have more than four guns out after deer at one time. Most climbers understand that deer have to be culled and that they provide food as well as employment. It's a question of balance. We respect that they have a right to the hill, and we hope they respect our right.'

From Mr Mitchell I got permission to drive up the private road to Luibeg cottage to let Nell Bynack see her old home. Off we went following the Lui and crossing the river at the Black Bridge, the green flats sprinkled with the ruins of the former crofting townships where cattle were grazing. A new Land-Rover track branched off at the plantation just before Derry Lodge, crossed the Lui and led right to the door of Luibeg cottage.

33

Luibeg, the house Nell Bynack lived in from 1912 to 1925, at 1,400 ft. the highest keeper's house in the Cairngorms and nearest to Ben Macdhui. The small building to the left of the house is the 'bothy' let to climbers at 1/– per night.

At the shuttered cottage there was a cry from Nell, 'They've taken away the brig! They might have left that for tired walkers. Now they'll have to go away round by Derry Lodge unless they can get across the river.'

We were on the edge of the Cairngorm Nature Reserve which stretches north over the greatest area in Scotland above 4,000 ft., arctic plateau, rocky corries with high lochans and glens of great character such as the Feshie, Luibeg and the Derry.

Nell was filling her eyes with the features she remembered so well, giving me the names of the hills, remembering what the wee sheds were used for in her day. 'Now there's nobody.' Not quite, however, as a climber appeared at the door of the bothy and invited us in for a warm at the fire and a mug of tea.

He was Arthur Paul, Creag Dhu Mountaineering Club man, and soon Nell was ensconced in the armchair of honour, seeing how the bothymen live – and very comfortably, too, I may say. Arthur Paul represents the new breed of very hard climbers who are pushing further the frontiers of technique, as did Tom Patey in his day from this very bothy when Bob Scott was in his heyday as keeper of the Derry.

I wrote about Bob in 'My Month' in February when I hoped that in his retirement to a cottage near Mar Lodge he'd be spared for many a day to come. Bob was ill when I wrote that and shortly afterwards he went into hospital enduring much suffering. Sorrowfully I have to report that he was buried in Braemar on 30 July. So long as there is a bothy here his name will be remembered as its father-figure, gruff, kindly and full of wisdom. The deep love that Nell had for the Bynack, Bob had for Luibeg.

I would have taken Nell to the Bynack as well if we'd been able to drive across the Geldie. I'd been in it in the '30s when the house was in reasonably good shape before the vandals tore up the place for firewood. Now I was to see it by helicopter on a windy day of low cloud on the hills, but the Dee valley was in sunshine when we took off from Crathie, with special permission from Balmoral Estate.

To say the flight was bumpy is putting it mildly. It was easy enough for me, provided I could keep down my breakfast, but difficult for the film cameraman who sits at the opening normally covered by a door on the side of the machine. My job was to select the route and choose the subjects for photography, after which the pilot would manoeuvre the helicopter into the sweeps which would enable the cameraman to get to work.

The glorious feature of the Dee valley between Balmoral and Braemar is the way the wooded bluffs are disposed on the winding river backed by heather hills. Keeping fairly low we found it just a bit too rough for comfort and decided to go on upstream to the junction of the Dee with the Geldie to see how things were there, looking to the wee plantation at Bynack, the green flats and the footpath going south to the Tilt.

I saw some really resourceful flying as the pilot turned the helicopter and flew side-on, dropping height so that we appeared to be skimming the river like a sandpiper. For the first time I realised what a crofting population this area must have carried, judging by the number of ruins peppering the flats between the White Bridge and the Linn of Dee: Gaelic-speaking people who gave up the struggle to win a living from the land in this meeting place of long cross-country paths.

Then into the pines at the Linn of Dee where the river almost disappears from sight between gorge walls that seem to touch when viewed from the air. The white gush of water is lost in the cavernous depth of the grey rocks and beer brown pools where the salmon wait to jump and otters sometimes lurk to catch them.

After that we swung over the village of Inverey and then looked down on the massive buttresses and red roof tiles of Mar Lodge to the gravelly river junction of the Quoich with the Dee. Hovering and turning slowly for a camera pan we turned north-west for the lovely glen that is the approach to Beinn a' Bhuird, skimming the tops of the Caledonian pines and hanging like a kestrel over the Linn of Quoich above the Earl of Mar's Punchbowl.

We could see the dark hole in the rocks by the waterfall, the scene on 27 August 1715 of a great gathering of hunters ostensibly out on a deer drive and every one of them a dedicated Jacobite. Rob Roy was there among a few hundred guests plotting to dethrone George I of Hanover, otherwise known as German Geordie, and put King James VIII on the throne. To toast success they filled the pot-hole on the riverside with 'ankers of acquavitae' to drink success to the 1715 Rising. Sadly, their high hopes perished at Sheriffmuir, but it didn't prevent the men of Mar rising again to follow Prince Charlie in 1745.

I love the story of Peter Grant, the Mar sergeant-major who at 107 was the last survivor of the '45 Rising. Captured at Culloden and taken to Carlisle where many Jacobites faced execution, Peter managed the almost impossible feat of escaping by simply climbing the castle walls in the dark to walk all the way back to Deeside.

George IV was told Peter's story in 1822 when the monarch paid his historic visit to Edinburgh. The King's reaction was to grant Peter a pension of a guinea a week for life, adding that payment should be put into effect as quickly as possible in case the old man didn't get the full benefit. On being told that he was being granted the pension as the King's oldest subject, Peter is reported to have replied, 'Aye, and the oldest rebel.' At his death, aged 110, his oldest friend, aged 90, played the bagpipes and the tune was 'Wha widna fecht for Charlie's right?'

Peter is buried in the old cemetery beside Braemar Castle, and I had a completely new impression of Braemar's superb setting as we helicoptered in from the west. There was the graceful curve where three rivers meet in a mile, the Clunie coming down from the south and the Slugain from the north, uniting with the Dee under the wooded bluffs of Creag Choinnich on one side and Creag a Chleirich on the other with an impression of an alpine hamlet cupped between them, its centrepiece the little green oval of the Games Park.

Now we swung away towards the Old Bridge of Dee across Ballochbuie, seeing the thriving wee pines regenerating inside the deer fences put up by the Balmoral Estate to ensure continuance of this most marvellous piece of primeval forest in Scotland, miraculously saved from the axe when Queen Victoria fell in love with Deeside and in time

The Caledonian pine forest of Ballochbuie. Queen Victoria called it 'The bonniest plaid in Scotland'. She saved it from being felled by the Royal purchase of Balmoral and renting the wood until she was able to buy it.

negotiated the purchase of the wood in 1878. She celebrated by building a cairn on Craig Doin bearing words which nobody can fault, 'The Bonniest Plaid in Scotland'.

Marvellous as all this was, I have to admit I was glad when we landed, for the buffeting of the wind was rather akin to being in a small boat on a rough sea. Curiously, though, flying had been much steadier away from the Dee valley, so the configuration of the picturesque bluffs hemming the river must have something to do with it.

After that I was glad to set off on foot and pay a visit to a wee farm called Ardoch, which means 'High Place', with a stunning view over Balmoral to Lochnagar and the best of Deeside. Rob Bain, whose living is in 300 sheep and a few beef cattle, was coming off the hill as I went up to ask him what it is like to farm such a high place on your own.

Weatherbeaten, fit and in his early fifties, he considered the question with a humorous twinkle in his eyes. Again I have to paraphrase the rich Aberdeenshire dialect. 'You manage the best way you can. I'm fit for nothing else. It's hard right enough. I don't see anybody else doing it once I'm gone. I'm about the last in a place like this, at 1,500 ft., without much of a road up to it. The house is old and needs a lot done to it. Where I was born at Daldownie, a few miles from here up at the Gairn and another high place, there's not an occupied farm. The last farmer left a few years ago. I think he's in Glasgow now.'

Also at Ardoch is Rob's mother, aged 90, too deaf unfortunately to hold a conversation, but with a rare distinction which made me eager to meet her. 'Yes, they say she's the last native speaker of Deeside Gaelic. The language held on in the remote places, but when the crofting folk gave up for easier ways of living it died out. I don't speak it myself.'

The fine old lady gave me a phrase or two from her seat by the kitchen range where she and the cat were warming themselves. She got up to make some tea. 'She still cuts sticks and does jobs about the house,' said Rob. 'She enjoys herself.'*

I think Rob does, too. Many would envy what they have – a kind of inner contentment which is rare and not usually found with money. I think living close to nature and that marvellous view must have something to do with it.

* Mrs Bain died in her 94th year in 1984 and Rob misses her greatly.

THE BATTLE FOR JOCK'S ROAD

NORMALLY I GO another way if I see a big party on my chosen hill, but not that morning in Glen Doll. In fact, I had been hoping for a crowd, but not really expecting to see one at the remote head of Glen Clova where Glen Doll branches off. However, mine host, Jim Cosgrove of Letham in Angus, was confident that Scottish Youth Hostel publicity would do the trick. As soon as we turned up the track to Glen Doll we saw he was right: the two car parks were packed, with more vehicles still trying to squeeze in. They had come to celebrate with me a Scottish Rights of Way Society victory over a possessive landlord exactly a century ago.

The man in question was Duncan Macpherson, a Scot who had made his fortune in Australia and bought Glen Doll House in 1883 as a lodge for deer stalking. Soon he began turning back those trying to use Jock's Road, the 18-mile path between Clova and Braemar.

This was when the Scottish Rights of Way Society stepped in – quite literally. A party of four hammered in a signpost pointing to the path to Braemar, then one of them addressed the landlord. The spokesman was a notary public and delivered what he had to say in the official manner known as 'taking instruments', a formal recording of an obstruction to a public route by a private owner.

They were allowed to pass, but Macpherson later removed the signpost and continued to turn back walkers. The Society then brought a case before the Court of Session against Macpherson and Colonel Farquharson of Invercauld who neighboured him at the Deeside end of the route. The onus was now on the landlords to prove there was no right of way over their ground. Farquharson promptly withdrew his objection, but Macpherson used every device to have the case dismissed.

39

Jock's Road walkers begin gathering at Glen Doll Youth Hostel to celebrate a Right of Way victory over a possessive landowner.

Fortunately the Society was able to call upon 57 users of the route as witnesses. After two long years of litigation, and an appeal to the House of Lords, Lord Kinnear's judgement was that the earlier use of the route could not be imputed merely to the tolerance of the proprietors. He found that Glen Doll was the natural and direct route from Braemar and farther north to the fairs of the south. That judgement was upheld on 6 July 1887. (Macpherson's appeal to the Lords was rejected in 1888.) The Society was awarded judicial expenses, at a cost to Macpherson of £5,000.

What better place to celebrate this courageous victory than at Glen Doll Youth Hostel, the former shooting lodge of the possessive Macpherson!

There was loud cheering when the Vale of Atholl Pipes and Drums marched in to the courtyard of the Hostel where a Scottish Rights of Way publications stand and microphone had been set up for the speakers. SYHA Chairman Philip Lawson welcomed the walkers; Rights of Way Chairman Lex Watson thanked the Youth Hostels Association for their organisation and introduced me as leader of the Jock's Road walk.

What I wanted to stress was the splendid record of the Rights of Way Society in recording, waymarking, safeguarding and winning disputes despite a small membership and a tiny subscription held at 50 pence until recent times. 'But,' I said, 'it's the future we've got to think about now,

Vale of Atholl Pipes and Drums march in to head the procession of over 200 outdoor folk.

with fragmentation of estates, the tremendous growth of forestry and large scale mechanisation of farming which can change the face of the land so quickly. Events move so rapidly and secretly that a path can be damaged or lost before you know it. It's happening all the time.

'The Society needs a much bigger membership of active outdoor folk, especially young blood, or it will die, so join and add to its strength. Take a look at the maps on the stall, specially drawn to show the most important cross-country routes, very cheap, but invaluable.

'Now it's time we set off. There's an old saying that a good companion shortens the longest mile, and I know I'm in good company today.'

At that the drums rolled, the pipes blew, and I only wished I had a whirling mace as I headed a parade of about 300 of all ages up the Forestry Commission track hemmed by spruces which were tiny seedlings when I first walked this way over 20 years ago. I think the forest complements the first two miles most beautifully, giving greater impact to the craggy tops each side of the White Water when the view to the cleft of the pass opens out.

Out ahead was the 21-man Tayside Mountain Rescue Team, the youngest was 22, the oldest, 56. With walkie-talkie radios and two stretchers they were well prepared. There was also Bob Aitken of the Footpath Management Project, to see what effects the boots of all these people would have on the ground.

41

Bob had gone on ahead to Davie Glen's shelter, near the plaque on the rock which commemorates five members of the Universal Hiking Club who died on the pass at New Year 1959, caught by a ferocious blizzard on their way over from the Braemar side. The route goes to 3,000 ft., and the mountain rescue team were strategically placed to have it all under surveillance. It can be winter any day on the Scottish hills.

The steepest bit of the southern side of Jock's Road is just before Davie's shelter where the rocky narrows come to an end. Bob, the path inspector, didn't go higher than this, because he imagined not so many would go farther. In fact, over half went to the top, though most stopped for lunch among the big boulders here, enjoying the outlook.

It was a good chance to meet up with some of the company. I was glad to find a couple of Border hillwalkers, with a seven-year-old son, who was no odd youngster out, for there were quite a few family parties. Bob counted 240 heads, and Ross Farrel, the Rescue Team leader who was in radio contact with his men on the misty heights, suggested we should make Crow Cragies the limit of our climb.

It was a reasonable precaution, since the path is not very definite beyond the Crag to Tolmount. Actually it was the first time I had been here in summer. My memory of it in winter was of an arctic place, with the Cairngorms stretching like an ice-cap ahead, their soup-plate corries dimpled in dark shadow on a day when the glens were freezing cold. I was on skis then and enraptured by the unexpected activity: ptarmigan in winter white everywhere, strutting about, tails cocked like barnyard hens croaking to each other in courtship sounds; red grouse intermingled with them, and even the red deer had climbed on to the warm tops out of the sunless glens. My diary records that we were on the top at 2 p.m. and so superb was the fast ski-run down Jock's Road that we were below Davie Glen's shelter a few minutes after three.

Now, on this summer's day, I was expecting to be in a swirl of mist, but we had the surprise pleasure of a fine clearing and views out to Broad Cairn and Lochnagar, with tiny Loch Esk just below us. The Cairngorms were in cloud, but on the way back down the world was brightening, and I enjoyed the flowers, starry saxifrages, dwarf cornel, alpine lady's mantle, butterwort, wild thyme and many another. This is notably rich botanical country, especially Caenlochan just to the west of us, where Forfar's John Don discovered 170 years ago alpine milk vetch, yellow oxtropis, blue sow thistle and alpine catchfly. He put Clova on the map for alpine botany.

How nice it was to come through the trees and back to the hostel where a party atmosphere was developing, with soup, sandwiches, tea or orange juice for the asking. There had been no problems. Bob Aitken, who had been looking at the Jock's Road path before and after our mass assault, told me that he noted little change, except on the steepest points where folk tend to take short-cuts on the way down. As for the path itself, he thinks by reason of the cross-drains and stone banking of its outer face that it was probably constructed and maintained for deer stalking. Macpherson maybe did some good after all.

I was asked a lot of questions that day. One was why is it that our rights of way paths are not marked on Ordnance Survey maps as they are in England? This lapse is because of the apathy on the part of county councils who were appointed statutory guardians of rights of way in 1894, but failed to register them. It was no bad thing as it turned out.

The present position is that the vast majority of rights of way in Scotland have been established by prescription and are not recorded in any register. For this reason it is not possible to identify all, or even most, for depiction on O.S. maps.

The Scottish Rights of Way Society believes that if only certain rights of way were to be mapped, it would not be long before the argument developed that, as no right of way was shown on Ordnance Survey maps, no such right of way existed. The Society would deprecate any such development.

The existing mapping practice is preferred, in that roads, tracks and footpaths are shown with the footnote that they are not necessarily rights of way. Also the fact that no path or track is shown does not necessarily mean that no such right of way exists. Long distance walks such as the West Highland Way and Southern Uplands Way are in a different category and they are marked because they were set up as special ways.

To prove a right of way, it must be shown to have been in use for 20 years, and it may be lost in 20 years by failure to use it in that period. It must begin and end at a public place. It is a right of passage and passage only. The user has no legal right to diverge from the route, nor is the owner obliged to maintain it. A right of way is held not to be in use if the public have got out of the habit of traversing its whole length.

On any right of way path, no person has a right to challenge you to state your destination or give an account of your past or future movements. Finding a locked gate or a fence across a known right of way, a user is entitled to remove the obstruction to restore free passage. Don't just climb over and then ignore it. Send a report immediately to the district or regional council, addressed to the Planning Officer whose duty it is to assert and protect rights of way.

Planning officers often consult the Scottish Rights of Way Society whose archives go back to 1845 when the 'Association for Protection of Public Rights of Roads and Footpaths and Places of Recreation in the Neighbourhood of Edinburgh' was formed.

They were fighting to re-establish what had been public pathways across the Pentlands, and were soon engaged against the Duke of Atholl who was trying to close Glen Tilt. £50 was received from Glasgow and additional funds from Edinburgh to finance the litigation, and they won.

The Glen Doll fight in 1884 was a busy time for the Association under its new name, The Scottish Rights of Way and Recreation Society Ltd. It threw its weight into a dispute on its doorstep in the Pentlands at Dreghorn, and supported the Liberal MP for South Aberdeen, James Bryce, who had introduced an 'Access to Mountains Bill' in the House of Commons, to try to secure the right of access to uncultivated mountains and moorlands.

Bryce tried again and again to get his Bill through. He succeeded in 1939, but alas it was repealed before it was ever used, by the National Parks and Access to the Countryside Act of 1949 which does not apply to Scotland.

Thanks to the efficiency of the Scottish Rights of Way Society, and in recent times to the tireless endeavours of the late Duncan Macpherson (by a curious irony the namesake of the villain of Glen Doll), there now exists a unique record of rights of way. Macpherson traced every known right of way and drew them on a set of Scottish Ordnance Survey maps for use by the Scottish Rights of Way Society in disputes.

The task took this dedicated retired civil engineer three years, and in addition he walked untold miles investigating rights of way, and fixing signposts as way-markers where the routes were not obvious.

Money has always been a problem. The need for the Society remains because councils have generally not been exercising their powers adequately. First the problem was dealing with sporting landlords, then the Railway Acts, Hydro-Power Acts, new roads, and today's motorways and forestry, and new types of sporting landlords who would like to put the clock back.

There will always be problems and the need for vigilant eyes on what is happening in the countryside – that is why we need you in the Scottish Rights of Way Society if you have any kind of interest in the outdoors.

If you would like to join, write to the Secretary, Scottish Rights of Way Society Ltd., 1 Lutton Place, Edinburgh EH8 9PD. I'll be delighted to have you as a fellow-member.

White Days on the Black Mount

THERE IS NO doubt in my mind that the Scottish peaks are at their best when the colourful glens are free of snow, and the high tops are plastered white. Then the low light of the winter sun picks out the silver ridges and intensifies the shapes of the corries, deep in shadow. That was how it was during a long weekend that five of us spent, based at Inveroran Hotel at the west end of Loch Tulla.

By a freak of good fortune, the good weather began on the evening we arrived. After dinner we went out into brilliant moonlight and a ringing frost, and by the time we had taken a walk to enjoy the setting of Caledonian pines outlined against the softly gleaming snows of Stob Ghabhar, we felt we were going to be in clover. At dawn, the fiery sky, the pink flush on the snowy summits, the pale green sky, the crisp cold air on our cheeks as we set off, told us we were.

Our objective was the sharp peak of Stob Coir' an Albannaich, usually climbed from Glen Etive, but the lengthy approach from this side by Loch Dochard attracted me because it was so long since I had done it. It is an ancient right of way to Glen Kinglass which I've walked more than once, but I'd never seen it the way it looked that morning of brilliant colour.

I remembered listening to the roaring mountain burns rattling down their granite courses, but today all was silence. The waterfalls were frozen, and even the main burn in this notably watery place had more solid ice than open water. It was easily forded, and the normally soggy ground between the loch and the steep rise of Albannaich was rock-hard and easy for walking.

Wondering which route to take to reach the upper snow ridge, we decided to slant into the sunless north-eastern corrie. It proved to be

Loch Tulla reflects the snows of Stob Ghabhar behind the bottle green needles and pink-barked Caledonian pines in the deer forest known as Black Mount.

more time-consuming that we expected, on ice-runnels, frozen screes and slabs covered with powder snow, but it was a great moment when we topped the final steeps and stepped into the sparkle of the sun.

What a joy to be there, on a rocky ridge of granite edges leading to textured snow cornices, with the soaring point of our peak, flawlessly white! Down below, the weather had seemed absolutely settled, yet even as we looked, Cruachan's outline began to dim as a wraith of mist thickening to cloud moved across obliterating it completely. On the final rise we found we were sinking much more deeply than we had expected.

It was warm work, yet the wind was so chill on top that after a quick bite, we abandoned eating, and our fingers were numb as we tightened our crampon straps. With big, leaping steps we were soon down the steepest bit of the summit ridge, but the iced rocks lower down demanded care, and not until we were in the glen could we walk with ease. Behind us was the pink of sunset on the clouds which had formed, and two strings of red deer hinds crossed our path as we made for home.

We stopped to say hello to shepherd/deer-stalker Rab Alexander in his lonely house at Clashgour. Soon he had us inside at his cheery fireside and, while he was quizzing us about our day, his wife came through with the teapot and poured us out a nectar we will not readily forget. Rab hails from Cairnie in Aberdeenshire, and was at Dougrie in Arran before coming to Clashgour.

Chatting to his wife and two daughters I was thinking of an occasion when another thirsty climber was entertained by the deer-stalking family who lived in this house. The climber was Alma, wife of the seventh Earl of Breadalbane, who came in here after a long hard day on the hill. She wrote about it in her book *The High Tops of the Black Mount*, published in 1907.

> 'What a bright welcome met us there! The cheerful homely kitchen, furnished with a row of happy-looking little girls, standing large-eyed, like a flight of steps in age, and Johnnie, the one laddie showing signs already of becoming a strong and active man for any kind of hill-work. In the parlour was spread such a tea as only Claisgobhair could produce ... I am ashamed to say I drank seven cups.'

Rab's elder girl, June, is at Oban High School and is home only at weekends. Claire travels daily to Bridge of Orchy Primary and very rarely misses a day, despite three miles of difficult track to the old Glencoe road at Victoria Bridge.

The Black Mount, famous for its deer, had been put under sheep around 1800, but was restored to deer forest by the Breadalbanes in 1820. The lady who wrote so charmingly about having tea in her stalker's house shot six stags on one September day, yet claimed that the shooting was the least part of the enjoyment.

With a sincerity which I do not doubt she wrote:

> '... the close intercourse with nature – the solitude, the apartness, the constant variation of light and shade, the mystic vagaries of the fleecy clouds, the grandeur of the passing storms, the tender sadness of the setting sun leaving his last rosy kiss on the brows of the peaks, and the quiet peace of evening as we turn towards home.'

The hills were what mattered. Ironically, however, she gets the blame of bringing ruin to the family fortunes by losing vast sums of money gambling on horses. It is said she staked thousands at a time and lost. Her other extravagances were legendary. When the 1,000-acre Black Mount came on the market it was bought by Major Philip Fleming, whose main interest was restoring the remnants of the Caledonian Forest, with his brother-in-law Lord Wyfold as co-partner.

The estate is now split between Robin, son of the Major, and James, his second cousin. It was the old head keeper, Jimmy Menzies, who showed me the ruins of the house, not far from his own, where the most renowned of Gaelic bards was born, Fair Duncan of the Songs, Donnchadh Ban Macintyre who found his muse after fighting on the wrong side against the Jacobites at Falkirk. On his return, the young man was given a job to delight his heart, deer forester to the Earl of Breadalbane at Batavaim beyond the present road end in Glen Lochay.

The love of Duncan's life was the inn-keeper of Inveroran's daughter, Mari Ban, Fair Mary, whose charms are celebrated in one of Gaelic's finest love songs. In his courtship he suffered inner torture, thinking of himself as a poor unlettered man, while his sweetheart was of good position. Inveroran in those days was on a main cattle-droving route from the west to the Falkirk Tryst, so it was a busy place.

The estate has problems, though, which were never encountered during the time of Breadalbane ownership, such as the poaching of deer from cars when the herds are down at the A82. The carnage of dead and wounded stags shot by gun and crossbow has meant a night-time rota for the keepers in winter, patrolling from Glen Etive to Bridge of Orchy.

Another problem is climbers. It used to be that they came only at weekends, and many years ago the estate leased the old schoolhouse as a climbing hut to Glasgow University, on the understanding that in August and September users would come and ask before choosing a particular hill. The arrangement works well. The trouble now is that there are just too many climbers on the high tops every day of the week.

The opening of the West Highland Way has produced a litter headache. The scatter of disgusting debris is particularly bad around Ba Cottage. The present head keeper, Hamish Menzies, has a friendly relationship with climbers, walkers and fishermen, but wishes fervently that they would show more consideration towards the estate whose peaks, glens and lochs they come to enjoy.

Talking about these things in Inveroran after dinner, and stepping outside to see what the night was doing, we had to go for a walk, it was so beautiful; the temperature at 11°F and the full moon shining on a low frost mist in hollows, while above the peaks had the sheen of satin.

Next morning, thanks to the mist, the grass sparkled like diamonds when the fur of hoar frost caught the sun. Our objective was much nearer this time – Stob Ghabhar by its north-eastern side, which meant taking the path from the climbers' hut by the Allt Toaig in air so still that we could hear the beat of a raven's wings 2,000 ft. above us and snowbuntings

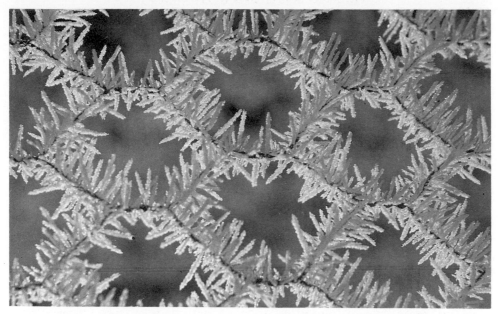

After a night of sub-zero temperatures the fence has grown frost whiskers.

chirruping distantly though we couldn't see them. We also heard voices and the chipping sounds of axes hitting ice out at the big waterfalls which normally cascade white down the rocks. Now frozen, they were providing a novel route for ice-climbers. Before we went out of sunlight into the shadowy north-east face, we decided to stop for oranges. They were frozen solid.

The classic route we were after was the Stob Ghabhar Couloir, a thread of narrow gully piercing deeply into the summit crags. As we traversed steeply to it with a frozen lochan below, we began to have doubts about the safety of the snow, which was unconsolidated. We feared the whole surface might slide off with us on it. From past experience I knew this slabby place to be subject to avalanches, for exactly 33 years ago four of us had been precipitated down that very face and were very lucky not to be buried alive.

I described the incident in a *Scots Magazine* article I wrote soon afterwards, lying with an injured leg propped up on a couch, and suffering from bruised thighs and broken ribs. The month was February, and it was May before my fractured patella was healed sufficiently for me to climb again.

We had parked our car at Forest Lodge, home of the head keeper, and what a tower of strength he and his wife were, giving us sustenance and helping us all they could before our late and tiring drive back to Glasgow. Hamish, the present incumbent of his father's post, was a schoolboy then.

49

I've been back to Stob Ghabhar a few times since, and by the couloir too, but the mountain this special day was to make handsome amends for its previous savage behaviour, as we stepped on to its glittering summit ridge, truly a fairyland scene with every rock encrusted in rime, frost feathers on every projection, and a diamond sharp visibility in every direction.

We couldn't tear ourselves away from the summit ridge, but walked about it for the next hour and a half, glorying in the changing light, as shadows deepened, corries became more pronounced, and the detail of buttresses we had climbed in Glencoe and Ben Nevis came into relief. It would be too long a recital to enumerate everything that was there from Ben More, Mull, and Colonsay, to peaks of Kintail and Affric and from Ben Alder to the massed familiar friends of the Central Highlands.

Climbers came and went from the tops, a pack of about 15 Holiday Fellowship folk led by a guide, two policemen out for a day, a solo climber, and about three other pairs. The pink flush deepening on the hills told us to get down or we might find ourselves in trouble if we were caught in the dark on the glassy ice lower down. The Black Mount had certainly done us proud.

Weathering The Winter

AFTER 29 YEARS on the southern shore of Loch Lomond, I can say with truth that the chief pleasure here has been the surprises that every winter has brought – and never more so than the past one. From an almost record low level of the loch in December, we went to flooded fields as the River Endrick burst its banks, then back to sun, frost, fog, rime, back to floods and then snow. It is a fact that we can have all four seasons in a single month or even just a week.

Of course, you have to be something of a philosopher, ready to enjoy the bad as well as the good, and my particular view tends to be coloured by the innumerable surprises I get merely by climbing Duncryne, the small hill that dominates our village and is affectionately known as 'The Dumpling' to local folk.

Like the Castle Rock in Edinburgh, it is a crag-and-tail, shaped by glaciers, and because the route to the top is by the gentle tail, you don't get the striking panorama north, south, east and west until you step on to the bald pate of its crag. Hastening up there one morning recently to beat the rain and view the floods of the Endrick which had burst its banks, I had a shock of pleasure.

The silence, and the clouds drifting round me, reminded me of the only time I've been up in a balloon. Through the different layers I looked down on cattle grazing in a field that looked vividly green. On the point beyond the yellow marshes the Endrick had vanished in an enlarged Loch Lomond, mirror-grey and reflecting black islands crowned with oaks and birches. Sausages of clouds moved below an even horizon of darker clouds enveloping everything.

Low mist lay level in the Clyde and Blane valleys, but the edge of the Campsies and the Kilpatricks stood clear, as did the lower Cowal hills to

51

Duncryne Hill, seen across my garden on a still and frosty morning. Villagers call it 'The Dumpling' – all 463 feet of it.

the west. A brightness behind me was the disc of the sun trying to push through the clouds, and as I took my eyes away and looked north again, there, above the grey horizon, stood the pyramid of a snowy mountain-top, Ben Lomond. To its left, above the clouds, appeared the glittering tips of Ben Vorlich, Narnain, Ime and the sharp prongs of The Cobbler.

The binoculars showed the peaks were really well covered, and that what had fallen as heavy rain in Gartocharn had been snow up there. I looked with new interest at the buttresses of The Cobbler's North Peak which, not long before, had given my pal Ken Crocket and me a superb rock and ice climb, landing us on the summit as the first flush of sunset began gilding the snows of this most alpine of little peaks.

That was a climbing day I would not have missed, nor would I have wanted to miss another outing on which I followed the loops of the part-frozen Endrick from just west of Drymen Bridge to where it enters Loch Lomond. It was my best local field day of the winter, memorable for the numbers of birds and their variety.

Loop after loop of river held something: pairs of mallard; springs of yelping teal, whistling wigeon; mergansers, goosanders, tufted and golden-eye duck. Whooper swans bugled, herons rose, jays rasped and fieldfares were constantly on the move.

Just 20 miles north from Duncryne are the Arrochar Alps, whose finest peak is The Cobbler.
Target that day was the North Peak, seen on the right above Ken Crocket.

The best bit, though, was within the National Nature Reserve, where since its inception I have acted as voluntary warden, making counts of wildfowl every winter month. This time I saw at least 1,500 greylag geese and about 250 Greenland whitefronts scattered over a grassy bump.

I was in the process of counting them, when from below the little bridge on which I was leaning came a high-pitched squeak. I had just directed my eyes to the sound when there was a faint rustle of vegetation, and up the bank towards me the source stepped into the sunlight – a water rail!

Moving daintily on slim legs, each foot placed exactly in front of the other, it paused, the lance of its red bill slightly down-tilted, sharp eye glinting, in a listening attitude. Not daring to move a muscle before one of the stealthiest and most elusive of reed-haunting birds, I admired its streamlined slimness, the warm brown of its mantle flecked with disruptive black, the dark stripes on its grey flank and the white feathers of its tail like a moorhen, to which it is related.

I don't think it even saw me as it did an about-turn and tripped back into the deep drain from which it had emerged. Another squeak or two from farther along convinced me that it might be heading for the spot where the channel enters the river, so I moved quietly down, waited a few

53

minutes and was rewarded by its slim silhouette as it came on to the ice and then vanished as magically as it had arrived.

Most water rails seen in Scotland are winter visitors, and the only clue to their presence is their loud squeaks which have been likened to the squealing of pigs. I'd heard them in other parts of the Gartocharn bog, but this was my first sighting this year. Previously, I'd seen as many as five in another place where they used to gather every winter.

That should have been enough for one glorious morning, but still to come was the loud 'clink-clink' of crossbills on the Sitka spruces, and a whirl of chattering siskins on the alders, not to mention tree creepers, a chirruping flock of long-tailed tits, and a charm of half a dozen goldfinches.

It was these hard conditions which decided Ian McNicol and me to meet at Killearn and drive in his car to Ben Chonzie. When I woke to dense fog in the morning and a fur of hoar frost on everything, my spirits were high. Within 10 minutes of leaving the house, the effects became absolutely magical as the fog began to disperse, especially in the Carse of Stirling as sun illuminated the rime on every blade of grass, tree branch and cottage roof.

Had we not had an objective, I would have gone looking for camera angles to portray the shining Carse as I had never seen it before. As it was, we were a divided party. My wife had decided to come with us and be dropped off in Braco to meet up with a friend, while Ian had brought along his friend Bob Cook, who has a plastic hip and had never climbed a hill in winter, so we needed our time.

I consoled myself with the thought that the rime would be just as good in Glen Lednock. It was a mistaken hope for there had been no mist above Comrie and therefore no rime. The mist, however, was on our hill, clamped down on the summit. There was a lot of glassy ice on the track, easy for us, but not so good for Bob who daren't risk a fall because of the fragility of his artificial joint. Accustomed to summer hill walking, his balance stood him in good stead.

Red grouse were cackling in the heather, and it was while up there, below the clouds, that we saw a figure in a blue track suit jogging fast towards us. I asked him if he had been to the top. 'Yes, before the mist closed in, so I got the sunshine. Plenty of snow up there,' he called as he sped off.

There certainly was, and we got the sun, too, as we came through the mist barrier and saw Ben Lawers and Ben Ghlas standing nobly above the grey cloud sea. All we had to do now was follow footprints past a line of

On Ben Chonzie, where the fence at 3,000 ft. was frost-feathered, a result of freezing mist. It was on this hill the party twice met a jogger who ran to the top from glen level twice over. I thought Bob Cook (right), with an artificial hip, had stretched himself as much as the jogger.

shooting butts to the wire fence which stretches across half a mile of summit. At the cairn, the wind was so strong and icy that we lingered only long enough to look down on black Loch Turret seen through a hole in the mist like a spyglass.

As we made our way back by a slightly different route, we saw away to our left a lone figure moving swiftly towards the summit. He gave a wave, and I remarked that he would need to keep moving if he wasn't to be caught in the dark. We were well down the hill when he overtook us and we found it was the jogger we had met in the morning.

'You again!' I exclaimed. He grinned. 'After I got down and had some coffee and a sandwich in the car, I still felt fresh, and as I had just enough time to make the top again, I set off with a rucksack containing spare clothes and food just in case of a sprain or anything unexpected. I live in Crieff, and should I fail to arrive home my wife knows this hill well enough to find me. It's our local peak.'

As this alert-looking man of about 35 made off, Bob remarked, 'You don't feel so proud of getting to the top when somebody does it twice in one day!' In fact I thought that Bob with his artificial hip had performed just as big a feat, but he has always been athletic and active. He summed up the day as 'Just great, and a completely new experience.'

The frost and sun we had been expecting to continue didn't last beyond the Saturday night we spent in Edinburgh for a day on the Border hills.

We went to the Manor Glen, climbing up the steep slope above Manorhead Farm, from greenery into thick mist and complete snow-cover, with nothing visible except the summit cairn of Dollar Law at 2,681 ft.

There had been a fair amount of drifting, so the snow varied from deep to frozen as we steered a compass course to Dun Law, then, with a fence as guide, changed direction for Cramalt Craig.

On the way, a swirl of mist revealed the black oval of Megget Reservoir, which we at first mistook for St Mary's Loch a mile east.

The promise of better things didn't materialise. The wind grew stronger, the driven snow more painful on the face, and by the time we had swigged some coffee from the flask and eaten a sandwich, our host, Robert Hollingdale, who knows these hills well, thought it prudent to turn back instead of struggling on to Broad Law two miles ahead, the second highest summit in southern Scotland.

Back we went by the way we had come until we passed Dun Law, making for the watershed where we could strike down for Manorhead, and good it was when the whiteout gave way to the greenery of the glen and a sight of the farm near where we had left the car.

As we changed out of our soaking clothes, I was thinking of the seven who were in a similar state to ourselves when they came off these hills in late February 1891 on the first climbing meet of the Scottish Mountaineering Club, first President Professor Gilbert Ramsay presiding with six members attending, one of them Sir Hugh T. Munro who was to list our 3,000-foot-plus summits for the first time in history.

The first Annual General Meeting and Dinner of the Club had been held in Glasgow on 12 December 1889 with 30 members attending, and Ramsay's Presidential address contained deeply philosophical words:

'The glory of the hills then, gentlemen, the beauty of natural scenery, must be our motto. But keenly as we are alive to this scenery today, it is strange to think how very new, how very young, in the history of the world this feeling is. The Psalmist indeed said in words, which are never out of mind, "I will lift mine eyes unto the hills, from whence cometh my help"; but the exact meaning of the words is open to question. It is certain that the sentiment of love of natural beauty, as an accepted part of our nature and of our life, is not more than a hundred years old . . . The early poets of antiquity seem destitute of any admiration for the wild, the picturesque, the sublime in nature.'

Later in his address he went on to apply to mountains what Cicero wrote many centuries ago about books:

'They belong to every clime and country; no race, no age, but has felt their influence. They apply to our youth a spur to exertion; they afford old age the peaceful pleasures of contemplation. They add a new elation to our hours of strength: they supply a refuge and recruiting ground in our moments of bitterness and depression. They are the ornament to our native land; they are our first object of interest in foreign countries.'

As one past three score years and 10 I say 'Amen' to these perceptive quotations, containing so much that I know from experience to be truth.

Alas, though, the wild and untamed places have been vanishing for much of the 200 years since sensitive people began realising their beauty – and although the present generation may love them more and more, everywhere in the world such places are under threat as man demands more and more from the environment and puts no limits on such demands.

All the more reason then to strive to preserve what is best in this marvellous little country of ours, and raise our voices loudly to resist unsuitable development threats and madcap proposals.

PEAKS OF SUCCESS

IT WAS 23 YEARS since I'd been at Tarbet in north-west Sutherland, and I'd forgotten how perfectly it is named, this wee scatter of crofts round a peninsula separating a fresh water loch from a sea inlet. At Laxford Bridge around 9.30 in the morning I'd taken the notion to go over to Handa Island while my wife did a ridge walk over Foinaven with climbing club friends. She had been with me on Handa in the 1950s when we took sole possession of the old house for a couple of days, enjoying desert-island peace in the kind of weather I love, showers and rainbows, with the northern world reforming after being blotted out by discharging squalls.

From the crowning cliff-edge we would crouch out of the wind, watching spellbound, a water-colour becoming an oil-painting as the blurred outline of Cape Wrath hardened to Atlantic edges of grey, with a curve of shining gold in front, which we knew to be Sandwood Bay. Then, warmed by the sun, we would relax, watching the fulmars and the puffins a few feet away, while beyond, waves burst round the foot of the Great Stack and our eyes travelled up the bird-crammed ledges with amazement at so much activity compressed into so little space in such nobility of rock scenery.

Everything about that long-ago visit spoke of an age before tourism, including the mere track leading to Tarbet, cork-screwing steeply down through rocks then suddenly the first vision of the crofting township. Magnified by misty rain, that vision had an element of magic about it, especially when we gave right of way to a couple of milk cows being herded by an elderly crofter, her knitting needles going busily as she walked. She directed us to the house of Donald who would surely take us over to Handa unless the squalls got too bad.

The friendly man thought we should give the weather a wee while to

The Great Stack of Handa towers between two headlands. Wildfowlers from Lewis solved the problem of getting to its top in 1876, for the first time in history.

settle while we had some tea. Lobstering, he told us, used to be the main source of income for the seven crofters, each with four acres of arable and a bit of outrun to feed 30 sheep and a couple of cows.

We had come at a time of mourning. One of two lobstermen in partnership was ill, and his two boys had gone out to lift the pots with the other, their uncle. They didn't return.

I saw how times had changed since that first visit as I drove easily down a smooth-surfaced road that came to a stop at a commodious car park, noticing, too, that Donald's boat-slip house had been extended into a restaurant. Handa is a Royal Society for the Protection of Birds Reserve now. Thousands go to it annually. Weather permitting, boats go back and forward all day. One was on its way now, which gave me nice time to make up a piece.

While I was doing this, a lithe climbing type stepped out of a car which had drawn up. Eyeing me with a friendly smile he came over and held out his hand. 'Richard Gilbert,' he said, enjoying my astonishment. We had corresponded, but never met. Richard and I had been in close touch during the preparation of his recently published book *The Big Walks*. As a guest contributor I had written chapters on An Teallach and the Cuillin, as well as providing some photographs.

Now I had not only the pleasure of his company, but that of his wife and two children as well, though we went our separate ways on landing, coming together just over a mile on, where the island plunges in sheer cliff to the sea as if cut with a knife. Like me, Richard had been here before, but neither of us felt memory had let us down as we gazed at the rock scenery and the ledges of the Great Stack crammed and yelling with birds. Then something extra, a ribbon of barnacle geese swinging round the headland 200 ft. below us, flashing black, grey and white as they swerved out of sight.

Richard and I talked about the courage of a wildfowling party who raided the Great Stack for birds last century. They were from Ness in Lewis and had summed up the geography of the big inlet behind the Great Stack and seen that if a long rope were walked round it, then pulled tight in a straight line, it would pass over the nearest bit of the Great Stack. Donald MacDonald was the fowler chosen to make a landing on the stack once the rope was in position. He hooked his feet up and locked them together so that the rope took his weight, then hand-slid his horizontal body along the rope 400 ft. above the sea.

As every climber knows, the arms are the weakest part of the body, and Donald's problem increased at the point of maximum sag in the rope, when he had to haul himself up as well as along. His movement had caused the rope to slip to the loose edge of the stack. He made it, with the very last of his strength. His breath back, he now pulled over the stuff for a block and tackle for the others to cross by breeches-buoy. They brought with them baskets to collect birds and a spare rope to safeguard themselves on the ledges.

I tried to imagine their jubilation once the bold deed was done and they were standing where no man had been before, and where no man was to stand again for another 91 years. Yes, that crossing was done in 1876, and Tom Patey, who repeated the feat in 1967, described their performance as 'a most incredible feat without parallel in mountaineering as practised at that time.' Tom got the bird, too, on landing – a squirt of foul-smelling oil from a resident fulmar petrel. Patey had traversed 150 ft. above the sea, a crossing that took him 45 minutes of hard, hard work, even with the aid of rope clamps and a leg sling to take his weight.

The next arrivals on the Great Stack came just two years after Patey, not by aerial ropeway but in a direct climb from a boat up the north face. Nor did they suffer the attentions of birds, for it was too steep for them to lodge. The bold climbers were G. N. Hunter, D. F. Lang and Hamish MacInnes. On the way down they abseiled directly into the boat.

Our boatman was from Scourie and as he took us back he told me that no lobster fishermen are left in Tarbet now, following another fatality.

Today Tarbet lives by tourism, the fate of all the dying communities on a coast where you would be rich if you could live on scenery. That night I slept the sleep of the just in a bed-and-breakfast house in Achriesgill, snuggling with pleasure in its comfort for I had slept out the previous night in order to enjoy the sun sinking into the Atlantic while the moon rose silver on the other side of the sky.

I'd done a pile of driving that day, all the way from Loch Lomond to the hotel where I had left my wife with her friends. Everything about the drive had been exciting, greens against bracken browns, the white of blossom and the yellow of whins, mirror lochs picturing reflections, the Great Glen floating a big white sausage-roll of cloud over much of its waters. I always enjoy the contrasts of east and west, as you leave the Cromarty Firth and its fertile fields behind for the Kyle of Sutherland and the stern wilderness country between you and the Atlantic.

Memory of course plays a big part. Visions jostle of long journeys by train to Lairg to link with the Durness or Tongue bus, rucksacks bulging with camp kit and food for extended mountain trips. At one time I had a fixation for the wilds of Sutherland, criss-crossing its highest and remotest parts and once finding a pair of red-necked phalaropes as I went to fill my water can for breakfast.

Motoring past Loch Stack I was near that magic bit where the surface is mostly rock and small lochs below Arkle and Foinaven. The mood was on me now to get away on my two feet as of yore, and where better than on a visit to Am Buachaille – the Shepherd – of Sandwood Bay.

My route to this hidden pinnacle jutting out of the sea gave me the solitude I was seeking, crossing a peat moor of oval lochs mirroring the sky, then over a ridge of hills into a world of little rock outcrops and soggy ground forcing many detours. I heard lonely voices, snipe drumming and golden plover fluting, but as I got nearer to the most distant edge I heard the roar of breaking seas – Sandwood Bay.

I could have gone down into that inviting bay, but preferred to keep high and turn south along the coast in search of Am Buachaille, which lies so close to the parent cliff that I had to be on the very edge to see the 220 ft. slim pinnacle below. Looking at the sea slunging through the channel between it and where I stood, I saw why my friend Tom Patey had borrowed two alloy ladders and carried them here to bridge that raging sea-gulf when he set out to be the first to stand on the Shepherd's head.

Tom was the pioneer of rock-stack climbing in Scotland, and living in Ullapool he combed the north coast for virgin sea pinnacles. Two ladders are one thing, getting them to the foot of that stack below me was another.

61

As I lay watching the sun dip I envisaged Tom and his two companions slogging with the awkward ladders for miles over the hills, then having found a way down to the foot of the stack, lashing them together ready for low tide when they would cross knowing they would have to be back over in four hours for the tide.

I could almost see the grin on his face after getting safely over the sea channel and revelling at being at the sharp end of the rope on unknown overhangs finding cracks for his fingers and tiptoeing along ledges on which he could zig-zag, pitting his immense route-finding skill against the odds of a fall. Alas, he died in 1970 just round the corner from Cape Wrath, after conquest of another unclimbed stack from which he fell while double roping on the way down.

Tom, the conqueror of Himalayan peaks, Mustagh Tower and Rakaposhi, Alpine climber of exceptional ability, with a record of more new routes in summer and winter in Scotland than any climber before him, did his last true mountain climb with me on the Cioch of Applecross, and he wanted me to join him for the attempt on the pinnacle from which he fell.

When the morning light came, I could see the bits of mouldering rope wrapped round the head of the Shepherd and the yellow nylon tape slings he left on belay ledges to safeguard himself and his companions.

The whole world was still mine as I traversed the cliff-edge to Sandwood Bay in the company of fulmar petrels, casting dark eyes at me as they maintained a parallel course without as much as a flap of a gliding wing. Sandwood Bay in the hard clarity of day had quite a different atmosphere from my sunset vision. The slunging sea was green, rising in white crests, breaking and racing to meet the golden sand.

I was glad to have all this lonely splendour to myself.

Yet it was welcoming to return to the coastal townships, houses perched above steeply sloping fields reaching down to sandy bays backed by a peppering of small islets, holiday home and caravan country nowadays, with Kinlochbervie as its metropolis, a fishing port that has grown considerably in recent years.

For the drive home, I picked up my wife and a friend, stopping to climb Ben Stack on the way, hearing of the adventures on Arkle and Foinaven, while other members of the Ladies' Scottish Climbing Club that day were on Cranstackie. What a lovely day it was to be on a mountain, on a fine ridge overlooking the Scourie coast on one side, with below us Loch Stack and the strange landscape of bare rock slabs called Druim na h-Aimhne edging a peaty world of lochans under mighty

Sutherland is most overpowering in its bareness due east of Handa, where the quartzite screes of Arcuil (right) and Foinne Bhein rise above lochans trapped in slabs of Lewisian gneiss with the scrape-marks of the glaciers which polished them.

scatterings of grey quartzite blocks which is the rough Foinaven massif.

We slept that night in the Spey Valley. I camped so that I could enjoy the sounds of the roding woodcock and the cries of the waders mingling with the songs of siskins and other dawn-chorusing voices. The weather held to the very end, with a delightful drive through Glen Lyon to enjoy its woodland lushness and tumbling river, a joyful place for a picnic lunch.

From the north-west I now had to go to Campbeltown in the south-west to present certificates of merit to 11 worthy Kintyre folk who had earned them. I had been sent an air-ticket to Machrihanish and was looking forward to the flight over Arran and the Kilbrannan Sound, but disruptive action by air-traffic controllers put an end to that expectation, and once again it was into the car and up the Loch Lomond road.

It was no hardship, with time to enjoy all there was to see, especially spinning along the coast enjoying sprays of seapinks at their vivid best and roadside banks of other flowers. Too many bays with ring plovers, oystercatchers, eiders and shelduck invited stops, but I managed to arrive bang on time at Kilchrist Castle, the home of Colonel Bill Angus, my host. He told me the form the presentation was to take.

'The idea was dreamed up by the Rotary Club of Campbeltown, to give public recognition to worthy people whose example can be understood by the young in whose hands the future of our nation lies. We intend to make it an annual event, but since this is the very first time we don't know what kind of turn-out to expect at the Victoria Hall. It could be 50, it could be 200 or more.'

He was to be presenting a slide show. 'It's entitled "Old Campbeltown". I've been copying pictures that go away back to last century. It's living history and it's fun. The audience will help to identify some of the folk in them, I hope. We'll break up the slide show with appropriate music from the local fiddlers, and with a bit of song and poetry. Your bit will come in the middle. Nobody but us knows who is going to get the awards.'

Any thoughts we had of lingering over a meal were dispelled as news began reaching us that people were rolling up in force and we would have to be thinking of a prompt start. First, though, we had to visit a hospital to present a certificate to Kintyre's oldest and best-loved citizen, Miss Mary McFadyen, aged 104, a retired headmistress who had lived on her own until two years ago.

What a strong grip she took of my hand as she asked me to sit down on the bed while the citation of her life of service to the community was read to her. Blind now, her face was full of animation and I could see why the nurses loved her. We were sorry to have to leave so soon, and on reaching the hall, got a shock to find over 700 folk seated, with more arriving. My old friend, the writer Angus MacVicar, was in the crowd.

The evening went with a swing, and all too soon it came time for my own speech, a chance to pay tribute to the many friendly folk who have such a sense of real belonging to a peninsula that is almost an island, from Tarbert to Southend.

The youngest to receive a certificate was Scott McKinley who got it for his bravery in the water when his boat capsized. He was an inspiration to his father while clinging for an hour before being rescued.

The last name called was that of the Citizen of the Year, the Rev. John R. H. Cormack, minister of the Lowland Church, an imposing, good-natured man from Tain who has preached and inspired the Campbeltonians for 35 years with his humanity, 'an almost superhuman quality which the awards committee sought.' The thunderous applause and cheering showed the popularity of the choice.

Conversation was good when we foregathered afterwards and it was well past midnight when I climbed the stairs to bed, but I was back home in my own house on Loch Lomondside before 2 p.m. the following day – theoretically to begin writing this article.

In fact the afternoon was so enchantingly beautiful that I went out for a walk in the belief that it would help the writing. I hope it has.

The unequalled beauty of pines and birches in the natural forest of Glen Affric.

Whooper swans and grey geese from Iceland make a foreground of National Nature Reserve backed by Forestry Commission plantations below Ben Lomond, the most southerly peak over 3,000 ft. in Scotland.

*Loch Avon, 2,377 ft. above sea-level, is a major glacial trench in the heart of the Cairngorms,
the most extensive area above 4,000 ft. in Britain.*

*November on Rannoch Moor, and the first snows of winter mantle the peaks of Clachlet
above Loch na h-Achlaise, in the area known as Black Mount.*

On the glittering summit of Stob Ghabhar on 29th December, my birthday, when every rock of the summit ridge was encrusted in rime and visibility was diamond sharp. On that day the Black Mount peaks never more belied their name.

Bluebells and yellow broom scent the air as in the last 50 feet of Duncryne Hill the view of the Highland hills suddenly opens up, Ben Lomond on the right and the notch of The Cobbler to the left. The Highland Boundary Fault runs across the nearest islands.

A brilliant moment after frost, and the Loch Lomond oaks glow against a dark background near the head of the narrowing loch.

Roger Robb on dry schistose rock on Beinn an Lochain on a November day when fog stretched from the English Midlands far into the Highlands, but above 2,500 ft. blue skies and sunshine.

A bracing day on the wild Sutherland coast of Oldshore with behind the rocky coast that leads to Cape Wrath.

The lonely splendour of Sandwood Bay, a graceful sweep of two miles backed by the headland of Cape Wrath. 'The slunging sea was green, rising in white crests, breaking and racing to meet the golden sand.'

Red deer hind with spotted calf in late May. As yet it lies up most of the day, the white spots effectively breaking up its shape. In a week or so it will be running with the mother.

A cock capercaillie in aggressive display. Largest of the grouse family and weighing 15 lb.,
this bird was ticking like a time-bomb and treated me as an intruder on its territory in Glen
Lyon. It drew blood from one ornithologist, and was killed when it attacked a Land Rover.

A golden eyrie on a cliff ledge contained a month-old chick, one egg which failed to hatch,
a feathered grouse, a fox cub that had been stripped of its fur, a leg of lamb, and a fox cub
with its fur still on. Taken in the Black Mount Deer Forest.

PERTHSHIRE PLOYS

O N A FINE summer morning in the sweet of the year there are few places in Scotland where I'd rather be than Dunkeld with a bike and my pal Pat for company. This edge of the transition zone between Lowlands and Highlands offers a wealth of bird life and undulating cycle tracks far from the artificial sounds of rumbling traffic on the busy A9.

Peace begins below Birnam Hill, thanks to the building of the new road on the west side of the Tay, which leaves Birnam and Dunkeld as delightful backwaters, with crags for climbers on Craigiebarns and, north of the Loch of the Lowes, a network of well-built estate tracks closed to motor vehicles except on official business. Plenty of visitors stop off at the Loch of the Lowes Scottish Wildlife Reserve to see the nesting ospreys from the hide. Few take the tracks that lead by a variety of routes to Kirkmichael, through country that was once part of Atholl Estate.

Pat knows this hinterland of lochs, rocky knolls, little mixed woods, marshes, heathery moors and conifer plantations with an intimacy built up over many years. He was in a state of particular ecstasy that sunny morning when an exhilarating breeze was bringing out the scents of whins, rowan blossom and balsam poplars. Bluebells were just being overtopped with new bracken, brilliant green against the russets of last autumn, and now and again we stopped to listen to songs of garden warbler, whitethroat, redstart and tree pipit. Walks up the steeper hills were always followed by nice undulating free-wheels, and the only pair of walkers we met congratulated us on our wise choice of locomotion.

Soon we were at the loch called the Mill Dam which drains from the higher Rotmell Loch with a marsh between, which we expected to be interesting. It was. 'Look, look!' Pat pointed, as from out of a roadside birch in front of us flashed a starling-sized bird in vivid black and white with flashes of red, a pied woodpecker flying low through a clamour of nesting black-headed gulls.

As the gulls settled down again, we watched through our binoculars to see what would emerge on the open waters beyond.

We didn't have long to wait before a coot nodding its white crown came out from the reeds followed by a quartet of downy black balls with red heads. Next was a smart wigeon drake, joined by its more sombre-plumaged mate, and then a teal splashed down. Beyond them were six Canada geese with three yellowish and fairly well-grown goslings.

On the bikes again we soon stopped among the rocks on the climb to the next loch to watch wheatear and grouse, listening at the same time to a reedy little jangling song from a birch-top above us. It was elusive, but whenever we saw the singer we knew this was the spot for lunch, for it was a good while since we had kept company with a whinchat, and this one was a beauty, its pinkish-buff chest and white eye-stripe contrasting with dark cheeks.

The other attraction of this spot was a tumbling of peewits crying their names against a shrilling of curlews and thinner calls from redshanks and sandpipers.

We climbed higher to be able to look down on the whinchat and wader activity with Rotmell Loch just beyond and I was opening the rucksack for our pieces when a large whirl of brown and white feathers above a pine tree folded into the shape of an osprey perched on its highest branch. We suddenly remembered our cameras, but by the time mine was out of the bag it was too late – it had gone.

Fishermen in a boat were casting in Dowally Loch so we pushed uphill past Raor Lodge, where a largish grey-barred bird was being pursued by a small one – it was a cuckoo being chased by a meadow pipit. It had been a talking point with us that this year had been poor for both meadow pipits and cuckoos. Perhaps the correlation is due to bad breeding seasons in the last two notoriously wet springs.

Our target now was Loch Ordie and its rim of rocks and scattered pines at over 900 ft. above sea-level. Here we got two more singing cock whinchats and half a dozen blackcock rising from the heather, Glengarry bonnet tails and white wing bars prominent as they flew below us.

Ordie is a big loch, but was so wind-ruffled that although we could make out goosander, mallard and tufted duck, there was little else, except fallow deer. We abandoned the bikes near the loch and took to the hills until time drove us back for a memorable cycle down the rough tracks back to the car where we were ready for tea from the flask.

We were back in these parts a few days later, bound this time for Old Blair and the Shinagag road, which was the way to Kirkmichael market when this upland country on the flanks of Beinn A' Ghlo supported several crofting townships on the limestone soil.

That greenness is very evident as you climb up by Glen Fender and reach Loch Moraig with the high farm of Monzie above at about 1,300 ft. Our route began on old crofting ground, as was evident from the ruins all the way eastward. As we got on the bikes Pat told me, 'You're following a route travelled by Mary, Queen of Scots in 1564 when she attended a famous deer hunt as guest of the Earl of Atholl. Over 2,000 deer were brought to her camp at Loch Loch below the highest peak of Beinn A' Ghlo.'

However, it was somebody else I was thinking of as we followed the rough track undulating around 1,400 ft. when suddenly Shinagag stood distantly before us, dotted with sheep and cattle grazing on each side of green Glen Girnaig. I was picturing in my mind's eye a blind man with a tin leg feeling his way with a stick to visit the shepherd pal who lived in this house.

That shepherd was Jimmy Stewart who served in the Lovat Scouts in the war, and the blind man was one of his officers, Syd Scroggie, who was blown up within a fortnight of the end of hostilities, but learned how to cope with blindness and use his artificial leg to walk the hills again. Until now I'd never been to Shinagag, and now I understood what a feat it was when, in February 1963, a year remembered for its long-lasting severity, with a 22-foot drift blocking the road, Syd and a pal used a marvellous day of sunshine to reach here.

We didn't go immediately to the house since it would have meant losing height and Pat had a hankering for keeping up the hill and maybe reaching Loch Valigan, so up we went by a shoulder of butterwort, tormentil, Alpine ladies' mantle, yellow trefoil, milkwort, violets and many another. Spanning a rocky gorge of the burn we were able to cross by a Himalayan-type plank bridge, very narrow, but set with handrails.

Pat had told me that Shinagag was no longer occupied, and as we came down to it we were surprised to see two workmen outside and a four-wheel-drive vehicle beside the door. The men greeted us warmly and told us they were employed by Mr Gordon of Lude, who owned the ground, and that the house was used now and again, mainly at lambing time. They knew of Syd Scroggie's visits to Jimmy Stewart, and of how he used to arrive from any direction – Kirkmichael, Loch Loch, or by the Girnaig from Killiecrankie.

67

I have my hand on the shoulder of Sydney Scroggie, who was blinded and lost a leg in the last days of World War II, but taught himself to walk the hills again.

Jimmy was a bachelor, an Atholl man, the son of a Glen Tilt keeper, a character who in the Lovat Scouts was known as 'Shinagag'. In a manuscript Syd showed me he had described him as 'a cheerful personality of bawling voice and rough and ready hospitality; his red face, bald head and single, tobacco-stained tooth, his dogs, pipe, whisky bottle, lambing stick and unbuckled breeks, as a byword for worthiness'.

The motto of the Lovat Scouts is 'Je suis prest' ('I Am Ready') and Syd in his service days with Jimmy had combined this motto and Jimmy in skittish verses. Here is one of them, by permission of Syd, who loved the man:

> *Think of the black-and-white*
> *diced bonnet,*
> *The buckled belt with the stag's*
> *head on it;*
> *Ready were you and ready I,*
> *Ready to scrounge and dodge and*
> *lie,*
> *Ready a soldier's death to die,*
> *Shinagag?*

I phoned Syd to tell him I had been to the dwelling of his old friend, and what I had found there. I described the views looking to the dark cone of Schiehallion and the Lawers range, gave him my impression of the Girnaig, and told him the only traffic we had met on that lonely track was a family of tiny balls of yellow and black fluff scrambling along to meet us. They might have done, but for the parents leaping up from the heather: a pair of red grouse.

I also mentioned all the old larachs dotted here and there that tell of townships that survived in these uplands that were divided between the Barony of Lude and the Duke of Atholl's land. Pat had lent me the *Transactions of the Gaelic Society of Inverness* dated 1978–80 which contain a well-researched article by John Kerr, 'Old Roads to Strathardle'*. It has a plan of the settlements in 1784 which were considerable north and south of the Shinagag road.

According to General Robertson in 1761, Mr Kerr tells us, the most considerable of his towns in the area was Shinagag. He writes: 'At one time the settlement here consisted of 35 buildings, three kilns, several enclosures and an inn. By measuring all the buildings, I have been able to find the largest, measuring 10 feet by 46 feet.' He presumes this was the foundation of the inn.

No doubt the shepherd of Shinagag, Jimmy Stewart, often pondered on these ruins and thought of the happier times when neighbours were within call and sharing a community crofting way of life. Wondering where he was now, I phoned Syd to ask.

The answer I got struck me like a blow. 'He's dead. He was murdered and the culprit was never found. Jimmy was found face-down on his bed with a hole in his head. He'd been clubbed by the marauder.'

Jimmy Stewart, 'Shinagag', was born on Armistice Day 1918 in the cottage of Clach Ghlas near Marble Lodge in Glen Tilt. He survived hard fighting in Italy, but died in a long and lonely Perthshire glen where you would have thought no harm could befall him.

I wish I had known him.

* This is also published in booklet form and is available from John Kerr, The Atholl Experience, 5/4 Sandport, Leith, Edinburgh EH6 6PL.

The Honours of Scotland

IN KINCARDINESHIRE following quiet roads from Catterline, I came to Kinneff, a tiny community with a proud story to tell. It was in the parish church here that the Rev. James Grainger stored the Regalia of Scotland below his floorboards for eight years until the restoration of the monarchy in 1660. The present kirk commemorates the event and I enjoyed having it to myself in the early morning.

In 1652, Cromwell was in complete control except for Dunnottar Castle, the only one still flying the royal flag. For eight months, English troops encamped outside Stonehaven had been besieging it, right through winter into spring, and the garrison inside were well-nigh exhausted.

Sir George Ogilvie was holding out against Colonel Morgan, but when fresh artillery was brought up they had to give in from lack of sleep. What was important about Dunnottar were those symbols of the Scottish monarchy, the Crown, the Sceptre and the Sword of State, plus some private papers of the king which the enemy knew had been taken to the castle for safety.

However, Colonel Morgan found he had been outwitted when he took possession of Dunnottar. The papers had been stitched into a flat belt and smuggled through the besieging lines by Anne Lindsay, a kinswoman of Ogilvie's wife. As for the Regalia, it had gone, and nobody would say where.

Its removal, under the noses of the enemy, was accomplished with the help of a serving woman who was gathering seaweed on the far side of the castle, watching for a bundle being lowered 160 ft. to where she was working. Into her creel it went to be covered by her seaweed and carried down the coast to the parish church at Kinneff. Tribute has been paid, in a commemoration tablet in Dunnottar to Governor Sir George Ogilvie's

This church at Kinneff commemorates the saving of the Scottish Regalia, which was hidden under the floorboards for eight years.

wife Elizabeth Douglas for her help in defending the Honours of Scotland.

The keep takes us back to Sir William Keith, Great Marischal of Scotland, who built it in the 14th century, and from this time onward it was the seat of the powerful Marischals of Scotland, who made Dunnottar grander as they grew in strength and wealth. St Ninian founded a chapel on the rock when it was a Pictish fort in the fifth century, and in 1276, Bishop Wishart of St Andrews consecrated a new chapel in honour of that saint. Twenty-one years later, it was to have a savage connection with William Wallace.

He stormed it when Dunnottar was held by the English, and in panic, the garrison sought refuge in the kirk thinking it would save them. Wallace set the chapel alight and burned them alive. A bit of that 13th century wall still stands with pointed window and cobbling, incorporated into the chapel of the 16th century which replaced it.

That incident sounds grisly enough, but worse was to come. In 1645, after Montrose's celebrated victory against the Duke of Argyll at Inverlochy in February, he marched for Stonehaven and caused the Covenanting Committee of Aberdeen to send their best gear and money for safety to Dunnottar. This was seven years before the Scottish Regalia incident.

Montrose had come to demand the surrender of Dunnottar in support of King Charles I. The Earl Marischal refused, and he was offered a

71

Dunnotter Castle, where the Honours of Scotland were hidden. When Cromwell controlled Scotland, it was the only castle still flying the Royal flag. Under the noses of the besiegers the Honours were smuggled away and taken to Kinneff kirk.

second chance to reconsider. It, too, was refused and Montrose took terrible revenge. On 21 March, he burned houses and cornstacks, set fire to the tolbooth in Stonehaven, burned fishing boats in the harbour and plundered the whole barony, but the castle remained impregnable.

Dunnottar is a peaceful place today, and without too easy access, for you have to descend by the fiddlehead, under a rock arête on your right and climb up again to reach the entrance door to the castle. This approach made a defence feature, since a watchman on top of the great tower could see people coming long before they got to the gatehouse.

To reach the top of the stronghold, you go up in a winding climb, the equivalent of five storeys, by the Magazine, the Guardroom, the Barrack Room and two access pends, designed so that each could be held separately against would-be invaders. The highest mound on top probably dates from Pictish times when it was a dun. I don't know any better place for a walk through history.

Back with my feet at ground level, I came to the conclusion that, for all our modern problems, we are a lot better off than in the more insecure times of poverty and ill health of long ago.

CHANGING TIMES

I NEVER CEASE to be amazed at how far back in space and time the connecting threads of friendship stretch. In last year's March issue of *The Scots Magazine* I paid tribute to my very dear mountaineering friend, George Roger, who died tragically with his dog Judy as they walked along the railway line near Bridge of Orchy on a foul day of wind and rain. George didn't hear the train nor did the driver see George. I recalled that he had been a navigator on the Atlantic Patrol, and spoke of the terrible injury he received then that could have killed him. I didn't say, however, that it had happened when he was based in Northern Ireland.

Recently, a letter reached me from a Bill Graham of Worcester Park, Surrey. He began, 'I have been intending to write to you since your article on St Kilda, the evacuation of which, incidentally, was covered for the *Bulletin* by my cousin, Tom Chalmers, then a reporter and later an editor of that paper.

'What interested me more, however, was your tribute to George Roger. Having served with 59 Squadron, Coastal Command, RAF at Ballykelly, Northern Ireland, with a navigator of that name I wonder if he was the same person?'

Yes, that was my friend George all right, whom I described as having had a great life climbing until well past three score years and 10. It's good to remember once more a kindly man and a great fighter who came back during the war after months in plaster when he had to learn to walk again. The story comes at an appropriate time as we remember V.E. Day 40 years on.

Bill Graham tells me in his letter that he was born in Drymen and attended Croftamie Primary, and later Vale of Leven Academy, travelling by steam train to Balloch and Alexandria before the line was closed. He writes: '. . . somewhere in the family archives there is a photograph of a school outing and picnic on top of Duncryne. There were three steamers on Loch Lomond then, and on a good day we could see them from our home as they were approaching Balmaha Pier. In addition it was not unusual to see six or seven excursion trains from Edinburgh, Falkirk and Stirling heading for Balloch Pier. On Saturdays I have counted up to 70 charabancs en route to Balmaha from Glasgow.

'With many more happy memories of the beauty of the countryside there, I can well appreciate your decision to take up residence in Gartocharn.'

Another flashback of a letter came from an ex-Lovat Scout, Theo Nicholson from Cheshire. Regaining strength after a sudden strangulated hernia, he had been on the 600-foot hills around him, getting ready for bigger things. He wrote:

'One of the joys of convalescence is reminiscence. I think I first met you in March 1948 at the bottom of Coire Cas at the end of a superb day of telemarks and christies on wonderful spring snow. At that time you walked on skinned skis to the top every time. The hill was bare of pylons, roads, buildings, ski-tows, etc. Those were the days!'

They certainly were. You had to work hard for your running, but the beautifully smooth snow was unsullied by the crowds of today. Nevertheless, I appreciate the recreational need for mechanisation in the '80s.

Then another letter arrived from Victoria, British Columbia, that touched me even further back in time. It came from John Macnair, one of my very earliest climbing companions. He wrote because he had heard that I had given him a mention in *The Scots Magazine*: 'Well, here I am as large as life and enjoying the delights of living in Victoria. Keeping fit and while not climbing anything other than the odd pimple, I still maintain outdoor pursuits, walking, fishing, swimming, gardening, etc.'

After telling me of a three-month spell in Japan and other far places, he goes on: 'While, as you can gather, I am very happy in these parts, my mind often goes back to bygone days – Loch Maree, our wee camps at Camasunary and Loch Coulin, and the magic of the Torridon tops. Sheer bliss! Do you remember Cameron of the Store at Kinlochewe and you asking for a quarter of a pound of cheese and of him telling you he just put a wire through the cheese and you got what came?

'Remember his story of fishing Loch Ba alone when he overheard three keepers conversing in the old tongue, thus: "Will we throw him into the loch, confiscate his rod?" At this point Cameron turned and addressed them in Gaelic. "I have heard of one Highlandman attacking three men, but not three Highlandmen attacking one man. What cheek, and me one of the best authorities of the old language in Inverness-shire." He was, too. The atmosphere changed. They advised him what fly to use and other useful tips.'

John goes on to tell me he worships the sun now and continues, 'I am 77 and a great-grandfather. Counting my many blessings I have a lot to be thankful for and so have you, attaining the lifestyle you so much enjoy.'

He adds a nice wee compliment that it was a privilege to share my early days on the hills. To that I would say that the privilege was mine, since it was John who took me under his wing when we first met near the top of Ben Ime. I was in a hurry to get down to catch the Sunday excursion train back to Glasgow, 1/9d return – half-fare, for I was small for my age.

Because of his baggy trousers and battered trilby, and the stick he was carrying, I asked if he was a shepherd. 'I live in Arrochar,' he told me, 'but I work on the railway, and there's no need to be in such a hurry. You'll get the train and I'll walk you down.'

It was the beginning of a long friendship with a far-travelled climber who seemed to me to have been everywhere in the Highlands.

By Jove, he could move! Lean and hard and nearly eight years my senior, he was a notable marathon runner, and thought nothing of getting off the train at Rannoch, walking across the moor to the Buachaille Etive Mor, climbing it, and crossing back to Rannoch. He had a tuneful tenor voice, and Gaelic songs were never far from his lips. He it was who introduced me to Torridon, half-fare for me to Achnashellach, then across the Coulin Pass to camp and climb rocky peaks of a quality I had never seen before: Liathach, Beinn Eighe and the Coire Mhic Fhearchair, Beinn Alligin, Sgurr Ruadh, Slioch, then to Kyle to doss out on the foreshore at Balmacara.

I was just in the act of writing this when a ring at the door announced another old climbing pal who knew John Macnair well – Bob Grieve. Bob used to meet up with him at that university of working-class outdoor folk, the Craigallion fire by Milngavie. Within minutes, Bob was recalling to me that it was just 50 years ago he set off up Loch Lomond on his tandem with his new wife, May, on the back for a round that took them 650 miles. With a wee tent, their honeymoon trip cost them £4, and he recalled how sunburned they were after three weeks of perfect weather.

Although Bob carries the title of Sir Robert, is a retired Professor of Town and Country Planning, and was the first Chairman of the Highlands and Islands Development Board, he is still the same man who

First Chairman of the Highlands Development Board, Sir Robert Grieve had a hand in the first National Parks Committee Report of 1947. He belonged to the first generation of working-class outdoor men, and saw the need for hydro-electricity, rehabilitation of the land, forestry and recreation to live happily together.

dossed in caves, lit wee fires to drum up and was proud of the fact that he could live like a Red Indian. He had just been giving a talk at a conference of Countryside Rangers, and had told them that if in his early days anyone had said that we would require rangers to superintend the countryside he would have regarded it with horror, scepticism, and dismay.

However, as he told the Rangers, 'Life and manners change, and in the course of time, responsibility fell upon me in various ways, in central government and elsewhere, to think very seriously about these changes and the problems they raised. The greater affluence of ordinary folk, the growth of car ownership, a virtual motorway to Inverness from the Central Belt, and our minor roads among the best of their kind in Europe.'

Folks who speed to what were once remote places have to be told, as Bob was doing at the conference, what a typical cross-section of the access roads used to be like, with grass down the middle and for wheels two runnels, pitted with pot-holes. He recalled, 'All the way to the west from Garve northwards they were like cart-tracks. I had twice to rebuild the back wheel of our tandem during our three weeks because it collapsed under our weight and the gear we had to carry. All that in 50 years. I've seen it, the whole thing right through.'

The pair of us have talked long and often of the economic problems of the remote west, and agree with the lines written by Leslie Steven that, 'Scenery, even the wildest, which is really enjoyable derives half its charm from the occult sense of human life and social forms moulded upon it.'

Over 30 years ago, the late Sir Frank Fraser Darling saw beyond the romance of mystic beauty when, as a great ecologist working in the Highlands, he wrote:

> 'The summits of the hills and the inaccessible sea cliffs are as time and evolution made them. The bare hillsides kept bare by burning and the grazing of an artificially large stock of sheep are not wild nature. Wild birch, oak and pine woods without joyous young growth, bereft of their rightful offspring by the all-consuming mouths of sheep and too numerous deer are not wild nature. Where woods have gone there are gashes and landslips on many a hillside, wounds in the earth are not nature.
>
> 'The Western Highlands are wonderful, inspiring, but empty if there is no smoke rising from the croft houses or vigorous young children in the schools. Men should be there, not just as tourists, but fulfilling their proper roles.'

I wrote down that quotation in 1947, and used it in the Epilogue of my first book, *Highland Days*. That very year, Bob Grieve, who was then working on the Clyde Valley Regional Plan, had, unknown to me, written the following:

> 'The climber should be able, after solving with precise delicate steps the final rock problem, to lie on the top, the rocky top, regarding with satisfaction work of rehabilitation going on below him in the glen, and the green stipple of the infant forest creeping up the mountain flanks.'

Both of us at that time thought that the Government was serious about National Parks in the Highlands, and would buy the land and manage it for development and recreation according to a plan which would integrate conservation and recreation. The National Parks Committee Report of 1947, in which Bob Grieve and the then Dr Frank Fraser Darling had a hand, showed what they had in mind by producing a plan for Glen Affric, which included hydro-electricity, rehabilitation of the land, forestry, and recreation living happily together.

Loch Lomond and Glencoe were two of the five areas proposed as National Parks in the late 40s. 'What we got instead was something much more piecemeal which pleases nobody.' The scene here is Glencoe.

This is what caused me to write at the time:

'It is estimated that more people will be employed in forestry than in the coal mines. The benefits to Scottish culture of this flood of life will be enormous. Into the bargain, the subsidiary industries of water-power and timber will be considerable. This seems to me a much better solution than mere development of the tourist or sporting industry.

'In the wild places, instead of grouse moors or deer forests given over to a few weeks' sport in the year, and housing a few keepers, we shall have, we hope, national parks timbered on their lower slopes, the glens cradling the villages, but all the upper mountain-land free to the wanderer. No doubt the sportsman will fit into the scheme of things, but in his right place, not that of a god. And I am certain there will be plenty of Scotland as untamed as it is now . . .'

The five areas proposed, and which were covered by a protection order were:

Loch Lomond and the Trossachs.
Ben Nevis, Glencoe and the Blackmount.

The Cairngorms.
Torridon and Loch Maree.
Glen Affric/Glen Cannich/Strathfarrar.

What we got instead of National Parks was something much more piecemeal which pleases nobody. Conservationists are on one side of the fence, developers on the other, and national responsibilities are shirked to the detriment of the environment. Instead of working together they have become polarised. Even as I write this there is a newspaper headline: – 'HIGHLANDS MUST NOT BE FROZEN BY CONSERVATION'.

New thinking on National Parks is in progress at the time of writing in 1990, as preparations are being made for amalgamating the Nature Conservancy Council and the Countryside Commission for Scotland into a Scotland's National Heritage Agency with Sir Magnus Magnusson as Chairman designate.

THE FRIENDLIEST PLACE IN SCOTLAND?

I'D LIKE YOU to read part of a letter I got from a commercial agent in Glasgow. He wrote: 'Within the next couple of years, if things go well for me, I will leave the area in which I live at present, and move to somewhere really scenic and friendly.

'With all the travelling you have done, which do you consider to be the loveliest area, or place to live in Scotland, and which would you consider the friendliest?'

Friendliness? Well, a lot depends on whether you yourself are outgoing and friendly. In the country, sociability is regarded as a virtue. Withdrawn introverts are little help to a community. My own experience is that friendliness is pretty universal from Scotland's resident natives, less so perhaps from the sporting gentry and their minions. If there was a rating, though, for overt friendliness, I think the highest marks would go to the Orcadians and the Shetlanders. It was the warmth of the latter that offset the bitter weather of January 1979 when I visited Shetland for the annual fire festival of Up Helly Aa.

Scenic beauty, as everybody knows, is in the eye of the beholder; some like hills, some the sea, some like both, and for them I rate Plockton or Shieldaig, both in Wester Ross, as the most enchanting places, looking out, as they do, on noble rock mountains and situated on grand sea lochs for sailing. The disheartening thing about these villages, however, is that they are being taken over by holiday-home owners, so that half the houses lie empty in winter. Because of this, I suggested my Glasgow friend might consider looking at Arran, a miniature of Scotland with its own Highlands and Lowlands and such a big social life for its small size that folk I know who moved there from Glasgow and Edinburgh tell me they can't keep up with it!

Plockton's magical blend of mountain and loch puts this Wester Ross village high on the list of holiday-home seekers, as does Shieldaig on Loch Torridon. House prices are beyond the pockets of local-born young folk.

Laughs all round for a recently born red deer calf within the Ben Eighe National Nature Reserve. Dick Balharry holds the calf, while the Highland pony on the left sniffs the mother.

Arran has a lot going for it: golf, mountaineering, sailing and a rich archaeology. It is busy with tourists in the summer and quiet in winter, but with plenty to do and see. There is a music society and a natural history society, and, unless you are perpetually on the move, the ferry service is adequate.

What has to be remembered about the West, though, is that it is mild and damp compared to the drier and sunnier eastern side of the country. After eight years in Inverness, a far-travelled friend told me that it has the finest climate he had ever come across, not to mention its view from the bridge over the salmon river to Ben Wyvis, with skiing in the Spey Valley less than an hour away. Sir Frank Fraser Darling, who loved the West, chose Forres for his retirement. He liked its sunny dryness and the views of the Sutherland peaks across the Moray Firth. When the great mountain explorer Tom Longstaff retired, he chose Achiltibuie and he wrote in his classic autobiography *This My Voyage*, published in 1950:

> 'I have written this book in Coigach, the extreme north-west extremity of Ross-shire, nearly 100 miles north of the Great Glen. A true mountain country, aloof from the Lowlands, but within sight and sound of the sea. There is spaciousness here. Light and colour are always changing on hill and water. One is conscious of the continual movement of nature, in the sea, in running water and in the wind that drives the clouds in procession across the sky. In winter, Atlantic gales and furious volleys of rain or sudden splintering hail keep the air alive and exciting.'

Of course, the late Tom Longstaff was not only a medical doctor and explorer extraordinary, but a man of means with great inner reserves. I suspect that most people would find Achiltibuie too remote and out of the mainstream of life.

I faced the problem of choosing our best place to live in 1959 when I married and moved from Glasgow, where I was born, to Gartocharn on Loch Lomondside. My wife had spent much of her childhood in Cornwall, but had lived in Glasgow since the war, and was delighted with the choice of quaint old Quarry Cottage under Duncryne Hill, whose 463 ft. summit commands what I consider to be the most stunning view over Highlands and Lowlands to be had from any small hill in Scotland.

In coming here, I was swayed by an old dictum: 'Praise the Highlands, but live in the Lowlands'. It wasn't a blind choice. Over the years I had got to know this splendid area where the River Endrick enters Loch Lomond at Ring Point, one of the best bird-watching spots in the West. It wasn't a National Nature Reserve then, but the handful of enthusiasts, of whom I was one, influenced its future status. Mine was the first official bird list, and almost everything on it has been seen again, plus a whole lot more since those early days.

With me, ornithology and climbing have been in tandem since earliest days. It was the same with my best pal Matt of whom I wrote so often before his early death. We met on the Fort William train as teenagers, and from 1931 until the war we stravaiged the Highland hills with rope and rucksack, summer and winter, learning as we went along. The mountains were our teachers. For Matt, after prisoner-of-war camp, the position on his tandem changed, birdwatching taking the front seat, whereas climbing had the front seat on mine.

To him belongs the credit of first leading me to Gartocharn, and I can say after a quarter of a century here that each year of knowing more about one small piece of Highland-fringe country has yielded treasure beyond any I could have guessed. Certainly I still love to go to high places and explore new and out of the way corners, but I get a deep personal satisfaction from seeing the same home ground transformed season after season. Each year brings something different.

The house where we live now is not below Duncryne Hill, but on a windy ridge sloping down to a deep-set burn where frost-mists linger and put a fur of cranreuch on every blade of grass and branch in sub-zero temperatures, making a sparkling world when the unobscured sun lifts the vapours and the Highland hills leap near. In the hardest frosts, Loch Lomond and the low ground are often hidden in a pall of solid grey fog and it's then that the climb to the top of Duncryne can be a revelation, as you edge into thinning vapour, see the disc of the sun, then stand in the clear, looking on Himalaya-like snowy summits projecting like islands out of the mist sea, Ben Lomond being their Everest.

There is always a special thrill, too, when I see snowbuntings or hear their tinkling calls up there, completing the illusion that I'm on a real mountain. Over the years I've had some very good birds fly below or over me on this hill, not just kestrels, sparrowhawks and buzzards, which are common enough not to be unusual, but goshawk, peregrine falcons, hen harriers, greenshank and rough-legged buzzard. There were real discoveries, too: the first green woodpecker that proved to be the most northerly in Britain for a short time; a pair of bramblings which I thought might nest; the thrill of going up there at dusk one summer night and hearing the 'reeling' of nightjars and seeing their moth-like flights.

On the frosty morning of 16 December 1984, the gold ball of the sun rising in a clear sky sent me to the hill, but first I had a look at the wee marsh at its foot – always good for small birds after a hard night. Smiling to myself at the staccato trills of a singing wren, and picking out goldcrest, robin and hedge sparrow as I sought its stumpy form, I caught a glimpse of a very light-coloured bird which obliged me by darting down to the edge of the burn and picking daintily along its frosty edge.

Pale breasted, slate grey on the mantle, slim and with noticeable eye stripes, it was a chiffchaff, a migrant which should be in North Africa at that time of year. Never still, it flitted to peck at seed heads, darted up into the alders, dabbing, dabbing all the time and apparently finding food. Following it along the edge of the marsh, I put up four snipe, two wagtails – one pied, one grey – a woodcock, and found the single arrow footprints of a water rail – each arrow exactly in line with the other, as if they had been made by a one-legged bird, so carefully does this skulker place one foot in front of the other.

The chiffchaff puzzled me because of its lack of olive-green cast. It looked so unlike the sombre wee migrant which comes to us in late March or early April and attracts our attention with its silvery call of 'chiff-chaff, chiff-chaff'. The literature convinced me that it must be a Scandinavian or Siberian chiffchaff, found occasionally at migration time on Fair Isle.

It happens that Roger Broad, who used to be at the bird observatory there, is RSPB representative in our area now, so I phoned him. 'It sounds like a Siberian,' he said, 'but it would be safer to call it a northern chiffchaff. I reckon its normal haunt at this time should be the Mediterranean area. It will be difficult for it to survive so far north here unless the winter is reasonably mild.'

Nowadays I find the winters seem to get shorter, especially 1983–4. Even before the big blizzard in the third week of January, I was getting grand skiing on the undulating ridges between the house and Loch Lomond, on powder snow lying on a good base, perfect for easy turning. As early as 15 February my diary entry reads:

> Cold east wind veering south-west. At Endrick Mouth, 50 oyster-catchers in noisy flight, 300–400 peewits cavorting, curlews doing their 'coorlie-coorlie' stuff over their nesting marshes, a skylark singing. On the river a pair of goosanders.

Nature was bang on course to honour St Valentine but, just four days after that entry, I was skiing in Glencoe in conditions so icy that a cross-country skier slid down the Etive side of Meall a Bhuridh and was found dead next day. Skinny cross-country skis were not suitable, even for this experienced lone skier. Even on broader alpine skis with steel edges you had to be choosy where you went.

I enjoyed my skiing on that day of bitter wind and sunshine. Much more enjoyable, however, was St Valentine's Day itself with an ascent of Ben Vrackie on skis from the Kirkmichael road. Even to get off the highway meant overcoming a wall of hard-packed snow-cornice, after which we warmed up, contouring and climbing with only white mountain hares for company. From the top at 2,757 ft. the glow of gold sun on our icy world was impressive, especially northward beyond Beinn a' Ghlo to the Arctic Cairngorms. The run back to the car was exhilarating.

Every winter I get the feeling of living between two climates here in Gartocharn. It can even feel like two seasons, never demonstrated more than just before writing this when the Bridge of Cally-Braemar road was blocked by 18 inches of snow. I had risen long before sunrise to drive my wife to a rendezvous point on the Callander road where she was being picked up by members of her climbing club to continue northward for an ascent of Ben Heasgarnich, the Munro at the head of Glen Lochay.

Leaving the 17 ladies to drive on to their goal, I turned back to enjoy the dawn on the Loch Lomond Nature Reserve and, with perfect timing, got the morning flight of 2,000 or so greylag geese against the sunrise, listening to their discordant clamour as they whiffled down to a favourite feeding ground around shallow ponds that can be very good for duck. Detouring in the car, I was soon in a good position to approach unobserved.

The geese were nicely settled, not only greylags, but Greenland whitefronted and Canada geese as well. But it was the foreground activity of chirruping teal and 'carking' mallard, and hosts of wigeon cropping the grass fringe at the water's edge that commanded my attention. A quick scan with the glasses picked out pochard, golden-eye, tufted duck and gaudy shoveller. Then into view came the noisiest birds, 21 whooper swans neck-jerking in a kind of trumpeting water-dance. A heron stood near me like a grey gargoyle, a mewing buzzard was circling, and over my head was a great talking of rooks in the big beech trees.

I reckoned it was time I had my breakfast, too, before embarking on another local outing which occupied me until 4 p.m., at which time I was on a ridge above the house watching the sunset red flood eastwards and turn the snowcap of the Ochils a rich pink. As the flush was withdrawn, I watched the moon put a burnish of silver over Dumgoyne on the Campsies. It was nice to get home, light the fire, make some tea and await the phone call from Callander which would summon me to collect my wife where I had dropped her in the morning.

What kind of a day had she had? A tiring one, for the party had been on snow from the foot of the hill to the top. Travelling north they had run out of sunshine into fast-moving clouds in different colours of purple, black and grey, producing weird effects as they got the full force of the bitter wind. What made it exciting were the openings, for there was always a hole in the clouds in some direction and views were constantly changing, giving a feeling of height and depth that made it all worthwhile.

The only wildlife had been red deer, huddling on lee slopes to avoid the blowing powder. With such a good party of trail-breakers, the walking hadn't been too hard, and the higher they went the crisper the snow was. She didn't feel in the least jealous when I told her I had been in the sun all day.

So you see what I mean by 'Praise the Highlands, but live in the Lowlands'? I probably would never have believed this when I was young, but I am soft enough to believe it now. Not of course that the Lowlands are low. In my choices of places to retire, I didn't mention the fine coast and granite hills of Galloway, the splendid cliff scenery of St Abbs, or the friendly Border towns on the Scott Country where I've spent so many happy days. Nor have I mentioned Tarbert, or Campbeltown, both lively places on a peninsula that has been called 'finer than all the Isles'. Believe it or not, Southend is at the same latitude as Berwick-on-Tweed, but on the hills of Kintyre live the most Highland of Scottish birds, the ptarmigan, the only place in the so-called Lowlands where they are found.

FEBRUARY 1983

From simple beginnings deep and lasting interests grow. Witness the deep pleasure of an English husband and wife when they bought a forestry cottage in Wester Ross and by putting out food for a semi-wild domestic cat, attracted the rarest animal in the Scottish Highlands, a pine marten.

That was half a dozen years ago. Since then they have been making a systematic study of them without leaving their own living room. Not just one animal, but families of them, feeding unafraid and performing extraordinary acrobatics on a baited food pole. Now they can say with certainty that of all delicacies put out for them, including cheese or meat,

The wildcat (left) – the Scottish Tiger – is rarely seen, but Mr and Mrs Smith had a rare encounter. The pine marten (right), a rare nocturnal member of the stoat family, is becoming more common in favoured areas such as Wester Ross.

dead mouse is number one favourite. Also that the orange-yellow bib of every pine marten is its unique identification.

Mr and Mrs Smith have been corresponding with me for some time now and recently they had a new and exciting item to report. The story begins with a shepherd seeing a wildcat and three kittens sunning themselves on a drystane dyke at the edge of the forest. Then in January 1980, and again in February, the couple had glimpses of a large cat with a striped tail. They also had a suspicion that something other than the martens was cleaning up the food.

Then, last April, in the keen frost of early morning, there in front of the house sat the wildcat, rising up and arching her back and looking intently at the grass, ears moving like radar scanners. For a full minute she stood, then: 'Like a streak of lightning she pounced, both paws coming down together, pressing and holding still for a few seconds. Then she raised one paw, scraped the vegetation and brought out a mouse.'

Still holding it in her claws, she laid it on the bare ground, picked it up in her mouth, and in a couple of crunches swallowed it whole. Within a couple of minutes, after one false strike, she had another mouse.

It was around this time that they began to notice fewer martens coming to the window for food, only three compared to many more the previous year. Also, the behaviour of the martens had changed from confident to very much on edge. Mr Smith wrote: 'They constantly stopped eating, peered all around and often stood on their hind legs and sniffed the air for no apparent reason. We also noticed that no fresh youngsters appeared as in other years, even though two of the females showed bodily signs of having had young by their enlarged teats.'

87

Then on their last late autumn visit to the cottage the Smiths put out some fishguts – for the cat if it was about – and some food on the table for the martens, three mice, which they had trapped, plus bread and milk. Also some cheese on a frame placed high, so they could identify the marten by its neck pattern when it stretched up.

Mr Smith resumes: 'Our favourite marten, Quixote, came soon after darkness fell and was most excited by the variety of fare. We call her Quixote because she is always on the alert while eating and constantly stops to survey the ground below. This time she suddenly became extremely curious, looking intently for longish intervals at the side garden. Then she bolted, faster than I have ever seen any marten race, away from where she had been peering.

'As she fled, the villain of the piece walked into the window light. Of all the exciting wildlife events I've ever seen this was the most amazing. An enormous wildcat, sniffing the food and picking up one mouse, two mice, three mice, each devoured in a single crunch and a couple of chews. Then with bread, butter and cheese to finish, she licked the plate clean before grooming herself with her tongue.'

It could be this wildcat was hostile to the martens, and may have been capable of killing and eating a full-grown marten. Or was it preying on the young, despite there being food enough for all? Watching the wildcat eat, Mr Smith had been amazed at her intake of food.

The Secrets of Arthur's Seat

I HAD GOOD REASON to be in high spirits that sunny morning of crisp visibility as I drove down Edinburgh's Canongate to the Holyrood car park, for I was anticipating an unusual day on one of Scotland's best wee mountains – Arthur's Seat. The unusual bit was that I had a rendezvous with a trio of geologists, one of whom, David McAdam, was going to explain to me in simple language what makes the rocky little peak so interesting.

I knew Arthur's Seat well enough as a climber, of course, and was enjoying the sight of it that morning, brilliant as a colour slide projected above the Old Edinburgh closes, the pink escarpment of the vertical crags cornicing the sky and the raised lump of the Lion's Head lifting behind it; classic rock-scrambling ground of the first generation of Scottish Mountaineering Club men who, at the end of the last century, edged themselves up the steepest places.

Harold Raeburn* wrote in 1897:

> 'Though the climbs on the crags nowhere exceed 90 feet in height, yet even these gain a wonderful impressiveness from being placed on the summit of a steep talus† slope of over 200 ft.; and in a dense mist, when the North Sea haar hides the city and the green slopes below, and exaggerates and distorts the rugged basaltic ribs and buttresses, one feels as far above the world as on some splintered crag in a wild north-eastern corrie 2,000 or 3,000 ft. above sea-level.'

* One of the great early Scottish climbers chosen for the first attempt on Mt Everest in 1921.
† Scree

I can testify that the climbs can feel vertically serious; even the polished rocks of the Cat's Nick Gully in windy weather with the rain buffeting – the ideal conditions for doing it if you don't want to be caught breaking the bye-laws by a Park Constable. In severe winters when a great snow-cornice builds up and overhangs the exit, the easy gully becomes a challenge to skill with the ice-axe, as Scott Johnstone, one of the geologists in our party, was to describe to me later that day.

Scott, a climbing man, author of the Scottish Mountaineering Club *Guide to the Western Highlands*, had arranged this outing and he was waiting in the car park to introduce me to his two colleagues, David Greig and David McAdam of the South Lowlands Unit of the Institute of Geological Sciences. The Institute's Scottish HQ is Murchison House, Liberton, where they have a workforce of over 200.

In my younger days I was an Ordnance Surveyor, and I knew Arthur's Seat well then for I used to climb it every day when I was working in Edinburgh in 1946. My lodgings were above a butcher's warehouse and sleep often became impossible in the morning, with tramping feet and loud shouts preceding the thumping of mallets and banging of cleavers.

I had chosen the digs to be near the Seat, so all I had to do to escape the noise was nip down Holyrood Park Road and I was in the Queen's Park below the slash of gully known as the Gutted Haddie. Then I would make a choice of rocky ways to get to the top before the Park Constables were out on patrol. I am sorry to say I had noted none of the volcanic features which make Arthur's Seat the most studied volcano in the world. Now David McAdam was going to fill the gaps in my knowledge and the first thing he did was present me with two pieces of literature. One called 'Volcanoes', and the other a four-page leaflet with sketches and a brief text on where to look for the main points of geological interest.

'Don't be put off by the technical language,' said David, as we set off for St Margaret's Loch and St Anthony's Chapel perched on the rock outcrops which are lava flows of different ages. 'Before the Arthur's Seat volcano erupted, there was nothing here but a primeval sea. It rose from the ocean-bed like the recent one at Surtsey off Iceland, which is now an island covered with vegetation where formerly there was nothing. Here you can pick out the different lava flows by their colour.

'Let's look at this one and I'll show you how we know the eruption came out of the sea.' He scraped with his hammer. 'See how much softer this lower part of the rock is? That's sea sediment and it contains fossils of extinct marine creatures that lived in the sea when the volcano erupted 325 million years ago in the Carboniferous era.'

We walked over to the Chapel. 'When that was built 500 years ago the builders just picked up what stones they could find lying around, and that itself tells a geological story. Look at the different colours.' It was an interesting mixture, but who was St Anthony?

Research suggests that he was born in Upper Egypt in the year 250 AD. A seeker of solitude, he founded the first monastery in history. His saintly relics became associated in France with the cure for the painful skin disease called erysipelas, a redness and swelling which spreads over face and head. The affliction became known as St Anthony's Fire.

In the 15th century the disease was rife in Edinburgh. A hospital for its treatment was founded in Leith by James I around 1430, and I had noted with interest that this chapel looked straight across to the port. Perhaps the power of prayer in the name of the blessed Saint was invoked as part of the cure.

The mills of God grind slowly! Four hundred years were to elapse before a scientific cure for the painful and unsightly skin disease was found and it began here in Edinburgh when a young English surgeon by the name of Joseph Lister came to the capital to work with the great James Syme and married his daughter. Moving after seven years to become Professor of Surgery at Glasgow Royal Infirmary, where deaths by infection were appalling, Lister found the answer in carbolic acid disinfectant to kill the spread of germs which caused inflammation and death. His method was rightly called the Listerian revolution, and in time he was elevated to the peerage, the first medical man in history to be so honoured.

St Anthony had inspired the monastic life, and Lister a medical revolution, ending the high incidence of death after surgical operations. I didn't expect to find this connection on Arthur's Seat.

From the Chapel we walked south along the Long Row, with the green hogback of Whinny Hill on our left, a favourite place to hear the skylark singing. Below us was the wee valley of Hunter's Bog, probably a swamp where wild boar were hunted. Soon we were on a rocky crest with an ever-widening view of Edinburgh and its spires crowding the Castle Rock.

On the wee summit ahead we could see matchstick climbers converging on Arthur's Seat. The good day had drawn them out to enjoy the sweep of the blue Forth with a hint of a different climate to the north where the Highland hills were white, though around us the Pentlands, Moorfoots and Lammermuirs rolled benignly south and east.

We talked about the coal bings of the Lothians speckling the flat farm lands, and I asked if the tropical vegetation that became peat and mineralised to coal had formed before or after the Arthur's Seat volcano. David explained to me that the spread of vegetation followed the time of intense volcanic activity which started about 350 million years ago when the rocks of the Campsies, Kilpatricks, Ochils and the Edinburgh volcanoes were being formed. At that time Britain lay in the tropics, part of a large continental mass which had migrated north during the preceding 50 million years, after being formed by the coming together of North America, Greenland and north-west Scotland on the one hand and the rest of Europe on the other.

Down we went now to the Queen's Drive to stand inside the actual vent of the main volcano. David pointed out the blocks of lava, large grey stones embedded in the pink magma* forming the sides of the vent. He showed me the frothy surface where gas bubbles had formed, explaining how the super-heated gas acts like a nuclear bomb hurling molten material from the depths. That the vent is exposed in section is due to massive erosion of thousands of feet of sediments which covered the volcano after its eruption, including movements in the earth's crust causing the volcanic mass to tilt 25 degrees. The glaciers moving east across the Lothians were the last great erosive force, ending about 10,000 years ago. 'See these parallel scratches on the rocks?' he said. 'They were made by the moving ice-stream and show the eastward direction of the flow.'

Now we went downhill to look up at the mighty skeletal protrusions from the hill-face known as Samson's Ribs, each one separate from the other and exactly alike except at places where they had broken off.

These columnar basalt pillars are exactly the same as those forming Fingal's Cave, Staffa, and the Giant's Causeway in Ireland, their regular hexagonal shape and architectural form the result of the hot rock contracting during cooling. However, as with fine buildings, weathering causes them to collapse, and right now up on the scaffolding were tiny figures working on the face to cement the joints between the ribs. A fallen fragment was pointed out to me beside the line of an old railway track which I didn't know existed.

This was Edinburgh's first railway carrying coal from the pits south of Dalkeith to a coal depot at St Leonard's. Today it is a grassy road leading into a tunnel driven below Samson's Ribs. I took a walk down there, hearing of those days of the 1830s when passengers could choose where

* Molten rock material

Edinburgh's Salisbury Crags, with the Radical Road running up to the skyline nose, and the skyline of the capital below. Sir Walter Scott and his friends loved to stroll and talk here.

to get on and off without having to buy a ticket. The price was 4d for halfway and 8d all the way. No wonder it was called The Innocent Line. The carriages were horse-drawn. The only steam was from an engine at St Leonard's pulling a rope to help the carriages uphill.

Duddingston was on the railway and the Sheep's Heid Inn there was a good place for us to have lunch. The Stuart Kings used to stop here when out hunting the wild boar over 400 years ago. Their traditional meal, it is said, was sheep's heid, hence the name, retained when the inn was rebuilt in the middle of the last century.

It was my first time in the village though I had been at the lochshore before now, and I was impressed by its old world character as we strolled past the Norman kirk looking for the white cottage with the red pantiled roof where Bonnie Prince Charlie stayed after the Battle of Prestonpans while his army camped on the hill slopes above.

We were lucky in Duddingston to have a word with a senior Park Constable, Sergeant Wilson, who is an enthusiast for everything pertaining to Holyrood Park. He takes colour slides and gives lectures, and he was happy to tell us some of the things we didn't know: for instance, that nearly every house in Duddingston used to have a weaver in

93

it turning out flaxen cloth; that its most famous parish minister was a landscape painter by the name of John Thomson, a great pal of Sir Walter Scott, who was an elder. Thomson was so fond of painting, and made so much money at it, that he gave the name 'Edinburgh' to the wee round house near the loch where he worked. It was a ruse to fend off callers at the manse who could be told in truth that the minister was 'away to Edinburgh'!

Sergeant Wilson thinks that Edinburgh folk don't make nearly enough use of the Park, especially in winter when Duddingston is crowded with wild duck, as many as 2,000 pochard and a whole host of others, including the tame ones, coot, mallard, swans and geese, which come to the feet of the visitors. It is certainly an exceptional place, with a list of over 120 species recorded in the sanctuary.

How did Arthur's Seat get its name? The legend is that it was named after the ruler of Strathclyde who was slain in battle at Camelon near Falkirk in the sixth century. Another curious name is the Radical Road which climbs along the Salisbury Crags high above the Queen's Drive and I wanted to know how it came about.

It seems that the Radicals were West of Scotland weavers, unemployed and vociferous against the Government. Why not placate them by arranging a job that needed doing, the building of a scenic road to replace the rough path contouring the foot of the high crags? The suggestion was Sir Walter Scott's, who loved to stroll there with his friends of an evening, and no doubt the going would seem rough to him with his limp. The money was raised privately and the road built in 1820.

We branched off to it just past the Gutted Haddie, which only now I realised was another volcanic vent. Beyond, where we branched right, the clean crags rise as a vertical wall where the hard rock was quarried to pave the streets of London. David had something special to show me here. 'We call this Hutton's Section,' he said, tapping the base of the rock with his hammer. 'You've heard of James Hutton who's been called the Father of Geology. He died in 1797, and one of his great discoveries is in this bit of rock.

'What he proved here was that changes in rock composition were due to heat. Molten rock from the volcano has changed the former sea-bed sediments. You can see the overlap clearly. The soft rock has been baked. It was a startling piece of evidence at a time when scientists were divided about land forms we now take for granted.'

I had read quite a bit about Hutton, who was born in Edinburgh in 1726, studied medicine abroad, turned to agriculture and chemistry in

Scientists of the Geological Survey at Hutton's Section with Arthur's Seat behind. This Father of Geology, who died in 1797, proved that changes in the composition of the rocks were due to heat and that molten rock from the volcano had changed the former sea-bed sediments.

Berwickshire, then devoted himself to mineralogy, settling in Edinburgh in 1768. His far-sighted *Theory of the Earth* has been called 'immortal' by no less a person than Archibald Geikie F.R.S., one time Director of the Geological Survey of Scotland.

Hutton could not accept the Church's version of the creation, that the world had been made in six days. His own testament was: 'From the tops of the mountains to the shores of the sea, all soils are subjects to be moved from their places by the natural operations of the surface, and to be deposited in a lower situation.'

In a paper to the Royal Society of Edinburgh he spoke of the debris being finally deposited in the sea '. . . where they are consolidated under great pressure; then forced upwards by subterranean heat acting with expansive power, and thereby split and cracked, the fissures at the same time filling with molten mineral matter; and so the process goes on.'

Arthur's Seat had taught him to see what no one had seen before – and make far-reaching deductions from his findings.

The section occurs in what I think is the most thrilling bit of Holyrood Park, the dramatic rock curtain of the Salisbury Crags explored by Raeburn. David gave me the explanation for it. 'This cliff-edge was formerly sandwiched between layers of sediment, the hot volcano magma being squirted horizontally into the soft material and solidifying between the bedding planes. The tabular form is called a sill. In this case it's no longer a sandwich, for the soft material has been eroded away to give the cliff edge which you admire so much. It provides good climbing and good quarry material, too.'

No wonder the Edinburgh folk were incensed when, after a long lapse of activity, the hereditary keeper of Holyrood Park reopened the quarries after the Radical Road was built. In 1843, all was made well again when the rights were sold for £40,000 and the Park was given into the care of the Commissioners of Woods and Forests. Its area is 648 acres and its circumference five miles of as grand a piece of small scale mountain country as we have in Scotland.

BACK TO THE BORDERS

I ALWAYS ENJOY my visits to the Borders so I was pleased to receive a letter headed 'Selkirk Royal & Ancient Burgh – Ex-Standard Bearers Association' inviting me to propose the toast to 'The Royal and Ancient Burgh' at their Annual Dinner during Common Riding Week in June.

The only disturbing thing was that I was expected to give a speech lasting about 20 minutes – not an easy thing to do when I was so abysmally ignorant about the Royal Burgh. I thought it was time to ring my old friend J. B. Baxter who had first sparked off my interest in the Borders when he invited me to be the very first to walk from Galashiels to Moffat over a series of rights of way knitted together by local groups covering different sections, with the approval of Selkirk County Council.

JB understood my hesitation. 'Come down and we'll walk the Royal Burgh together,' he said. 'There's a bed waiting for you.'

True Border hospitality, the same, in fact, that encouraged us to undertake the 59-mile Border Walk eight years ago.

My wife and I are not likely to forget that adventure, especially the first 19-mile lap done on the hottest day since record-keeping began. Even on the Minchmuir there was not a drop of water to be had until we reached the Cheese Well. We were not only dehydrated and roasted by the sun, but plagued by buzzing flies for most of the way.

Afterwards we were admitted into the distinguished company of 'The Plodders', whose insignia is a neat crest with the date 1645 above a pair of boots and sprigs of heather on a tie or a scarf. We had earned membership by following in the footsteps of Montrose along the route he took after his troops were scattered by Leslie's Covenanting Army at Philiphaugh.

This photograph shows me at the 'Thre Bridder' cairns, which divide the lands of Yair, Philiphaugh and Selkirk Burgh, the farthest point reached by the Selkirk Standard Bearer in a three-hour ride round the marches.

The venue of that presentation was the Gordon Arms in Yarrow on a snow-squally evening after a round over the hills to Blackhouse, where we crammed into a barn to eat our pieces in the very place where James Hogg, the Ettrick Shepherd, herded for 10 years. I was to hear more about the remarkable Hogg when we climbed over another pass to come down on Altrieve and looked across to the spot where Hogg ended his days as a not very successful farmer. Only the night before, in the Selkirk Courthouse, I had sat in his wooden chair, thinking of the imaginative power of his writings.

There was a *Scots Magazine* connection, too, for in 1802 Walter Scott was writing to its Editor drawing his attention to '. . . a young man born in Ettrick Forest, and literally bred there in the humble situation of a shepherd'.

It was a jumble of thoughts about these things that decided me to accept JB's invitation on that very evening when I spoke to him on the phone, and off I drove eastward in a greyness of leaden skies and fierce showers. At Carnwath the landscape began acquiring texture as the skies lightened, illuminating white dots of sheep on curves of velvet green slopes behind which were the dark Broughton Heights wisped by white puffs of cloud. I always love the run along the Tweed to Neidpath Castle and the swing into cheery Peebles.

Beyond that I felt I was on the home stretch, especially after Innerleithen with the ridge of the high Minchmuir, and its wooded glens hemming you in on the south, and above, on the north, the more abrupt wall of the Moorfoots, boulder-spattered and yellow with whins. Hard to believe that in cattle-droving days the Minchmuir was once the only good road between Tweeddale and Selkirk.

At Yair Bridge I had to stop and look up to the misty 'Thre Bridder', the first of our tops on leaving the Tweed, the 'Three Brethren' being pointed cairns on the hill dividing the lands of Yair, Philiphaugh and Selkirk Burgh. This high point is on the Minchmuir-edge and is the farthest point reached by the Selkirk Standard Bearer and his retinue (of 500 horses this year) in an exciting ride lasting three hours. Four miles on and I was at my destination, Lindean, just three hours from leaving Loch Lomondside.

How nice it was to meet mine hosts again, JB and his wife Helen; a warm greeting, tea ready at the fireside, and I felt I had never been away. Before I turned in, they had told me my programme for the next day regardless of weather. My dawn awakening was the cackling of a cock pheasant outside my window.

Selkirk had not yet properly wakened when we drove to our starting point for the day, the Flodden Memorial portraying Fletcher with his captured English flag, the lone survivor of the battle who, in bringing the terrible news, lowered his flag in a gesture of grief for the slain. The casting of the Colours at the end of the Common Riding ceremony commemorates this act of over 450 years ago. It ends emotionally with

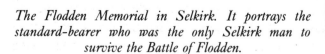

The Flodden Memorial in Selkirk. It portrays the standard-bearer who was the only Selkirk man to survive the Battle of Flodden.

'The Liltin' – the Floo'ers o' the Forest – in remembrance of past Souters unifying the present and the past.

To be a Souter you have to be born in Selkirk, and 'Yince a Souter, aye a Souter'. JB cannot claim to be one. The word, of course, means shoemaker, of whom there are none now in Selkirk, but it was a famous Selkirk industry, the Forest of Ettrick providing the raw hides for single-soled shoes. Their skills proved invaluable to Bonnie Prince Charlie's Highland army after crossing the Minchmuir on their way to try and take London. They needed shoes, demanded 2,000 pairs and got them, but payment was deferred, presumably until the hoped-for spoils of victory came their way.

Not far from the superb bronze of the Flodden Field memorial is the one in memory of Mungo Park. Both are regarded as among the finest works of the Border sculptor Thomas Clapperton. I knew a little about Mungo Park from his book *Travels in the Interior of Africa* published in 1799, the story of his first expedition, superbly told, a classic of dangerous travel. The monument is beside what was the home of his teacher, Dr Anderson, whose daughter he married after his first journey.

Home from that expedition he couldn't settle down, confiding to his friend Walter Scott that he would rather brave Africa and its horrors than spend his life in toilsome rides amongst the hills for the scanty remuneration of a country surgeon. In 1805, therefore, he was off again, to try to discover the source of the Niger, but sickness cut down the expedition drastically, and the final disaster was when their canoe was attacked by natives and all aboard were drowned. Today a Royal Scottish Geographical Society Award for distinguished exploration is the Mungo Park Medal.

I hadn't realised that the figure of Mungo Park stands where the East Port of the walled town gave admission to the Back Raw whose summit was the highest part of the ancient Burgh of shoe-makers, the tan-pits for curing the leather stretching up the length of the Raw. Up there was the Lady Well which supplied water for the townsfolk. JB explained it all as we drove to the Pele Gait, now called Castle Street after the castle that used to stand on top. From there we could trace the line of wall leading down to the West Port. I was impressed by the council houses in the area of the South Port, and not surprised to hear their layout and design had won a Civic Trust Award.

'You know what Selkirk means?' asked JB as we came to a cemetery gate on the slope leading back to the market-place, ' "The kirk of the shiels or dwellings." This is where it stood, and in it William Wallace was proclaimed Guardian of Scotland in 1298.' He took me to the tablet on the wall of the ruined parish kirk which pinpoints the site of the original building. Below it is another notice commemorating the fact that the maternal ancestor of Franklin D. Roosevelt, 32nd President of the USA, lies in the Murray Aisle of the present edifice.

This little tour showed me something I had not quite realised, that the old Burgh sits up high, and is separated from its mills along the Ettrick by a gey stey brae, which meant a climb for the spinners and weavers in the days before motor cars. I was glad to hear that, thanks to diversification into electronics, Selkirk has weathered the recession in the woollen industry very well – more successfully than most Border towns.

Thomas Craig Brown, a former Provost and very successful mill owner, is remembered not so much for his spinning of yarn and contract work in the making of military uniforms, but for his two volume *History of Selkirkshire*, highly regarded as a classic of what a local history should be. We took a quick turn into Woodburn House where it was written, now a hotel in its own grounds.

Robert Burns is remembered by another hotel, the Forest Inn, gone now, but a tablet on a wall tells us he spent 13 May 1787 here and wrote his poetic epistle to Willie Creech. Said JB, 'Burns went away with a poor opinion of Selkirk, for when he heard that the Provost and his magistrates were dining, he sent in a wee note expecting to be invited to join them. He was ignored.'

It is these wee asides which makes it so worthwhile to be taken on a tour by a knowledgeable local man like JB. I liked his story about Walter Scott as we stood at the Courthouse and looked beyond his monument to a shop across the road. 'During the Napoleonic wars Selkirk had 190 French prisoners billeted in lodgings with the townsfolk. They could go about freely within certain bounds, and they used to put on entertainments in what is now that shop.

'They were very popular. Scott broke the law by sending his carriage to pick up some of them and take them to Abbotsford, no doubt to talk to them about some aspects of their campaigns which would be useful to him in his *Life of Napoleon* which he was writing at the time. I expect you know that Scott's wife was French, which would be a common bond.'

We had just passed the West Port when my attention was drawn to a plaque telling that Montrose had spent the night of 13 September 1645 in the house that stood here. 'Did you know he was asleep in bed when the fighting began across the river at Philiphaugh?' JB went on. 'It was a misty morning, Leslie was in Haddington when he heard that Montrose's army were encamped in the neighbourhood of Selkirk. He turned about, marched his army fast, crossing the Gala, then fording the Tweed at Yair Bridge. Dividing his force on both sides of the Ettrick he was able to avoid the enemy outpost guards and take Montrose's troops by surprise.'

There is a substantial cairn in private grounds commemorating the Covenanters' victory, but however worthy their cause, they tarnished it by wanting more blood, and while the routed troops were fleeing to gain the heights of the Minchmuir, their women camp followers and children were put to the sword.

Where the battle was fought is now a sports ground adjacent to a modern housing estate called Bannerfield, an appropriate name historically, but the design and layout are an ill fit for the setting, and are certainly no credit to the architect responsible.

I had expressed a desire to see the birthplace of James Hogg far up the Ettrick so off we drove, stopping to pick up a man waiting with a camera at a fine view-point known as 'The Scaurs'. The waiting photographer was a friend, Walter Thomson, Editor of the *Selkirk Advertiser*, and he was delighted to hop in when we told him where we were going.

Our arrival was timely, for he was just in time to miss a downpour, but there were good moments between the showers as we threaded our way up the valley and through green parks of Cheviot sheep with their lambs, the scenery getting better and better as hillsides steepened and tumbling watercourses became white staircases, the best of them foaming down from Ward Law behind the Hogg Monument close to the quaint kirk near where the Hogg homestead used to stand.

It was the kirk that had attracted Walter Thomson to come with us, and as we went inside and looked up to the gallery running round its sides he began talking about the Reverend Thomas Boston, the preacher who, in his day, was so eloquent that folk travelled miles every Sunday, on foot and by horse-trap, to hear his sermons. 'His bicentenary was just a year or two ago,' said Walter. 'It went unnoticed in the Borders, but I got three different cuttings sent to me from Dutch newspapers. He was well known there from his religious writings.' JB reflected that Boston's philosophical thought could have rubbed off on Hogg – witness Hogg's powerfully imaginative work *Confessions of a Justified Sinner*.

For the drive home we went over the hills by Tushielaw, past slopes ploughed and planted with spruce almost to their tops, where circular stone-built sheep fanks are due to be engulfed when the trees grow up. Our descent on the other side into Yarrow took us past Altrieve Lake where Hogg later farmed and ended his days.

Down there we were entertained to coffee by none other than Dave Fordyce who had initiated us into the distinguished company of 'The Plodders' that winter day with the Border Hillwalkers, a day which had ended in dinner, singing and an entertainment put on by members of the Club with JB at the piano.

I learned, too, that it was Dave who put my name forward to propose the toast at the ex-Standard Bearers' Association Dinner. He was surprised at my apprehension, saying 'The Toast to the Royal Burgh shouldn't be any bother to you.' Being a Souter, Dave knows it all by reason of long familiarity, and perhaps didn't quite realise the extent of my ignorance of the town which, although only 719 acres, housing a mere 6,000 or so, has a history which encompasses the story of Scotland – and by its enthusiasm for the past makes the enjoyment of the present deeper and fuller.

If you live here, there is truth in the saying, 'A day oot o Selkirk is a day wasted'. That could be called a good definition of happiness in a world that could hardly be described as contented.

A New Railway and an Old Town

BECAUSE I LIVE to the north of Glasgow, I explore more in that direction rather than face the congested Central Belt, fast as the road-system is to the Borders and Galloway. These days it takes only an hour to drive from Bearsden to Wanlockhead as I discovered when I set off recently one Sunday morning. Pausing in Leadhills for a look round before pushing on the final two miles to reach the highest village in Scotland at around 1,400 ft., I was delighted to see a small well-built man, whose face I knew, coming towards me with jaunty step.

He greeted me with, 'Aye man, you hivnae changed; you're keepin well.' I said I could say the same for him, but confessed I'd forgotten his name.

'Jake Elliot. You were in the hoose the last time you were here. Mind we were speakin aboot the railway wi the wife. She was tellin ye aboot travellin back and furrit tae school on it, fae the hoose doon the valley where her faither was shepherd.' I remembered that bit. 'Are ye coming up tae see her?'

I didn't just then, but I did later on, and found Jake enjoying the bowling on television while his wife was busy house-painting. 'He's retired now,' she said pointedly, but Jake was quick to respond that he still helped with the lambing, and a gey cold one it had been. Once again, though, it was the railway we got round to and the aims of the Lowther Railway Society, who for the past two years have been gathering members and raising funds to operate a two-foot narrow gauge line at Leadhills and Wanlockhead on the former Caledonian trackbed.

Mrs Greta Clark had written in February asking me if I would do the formal opening on Saturday, 24 May. My intention was now to call on her

104

Jake Elliot, the Leadhill shepherd who in retirement still helps with the lambing.

at Woodlands Hall in Leadhills to see and hear how things were progressing. Before I could do so, she had heard of my arrival and I was meeting her energetic husband, Charles, who is an engineer in the water department and works in the County Buildings in Hamilton.

When I was last in the village, Greta had run the post office. Now she is in charge of publicity for the railway society, while in his spare time Charles applies his engineering skills to the engine and rolling stock. A large area of their back garden has been converted to railway works.

We had just started talking and the coffee had been poured, when Chairman Alastair Ireland arrived. Alastair was brought up in Glasgow, but since boyhood has had a long connection with Elvanfoot, and the Lowther Hills where he used to grouse-beat in his summer holidays. Three generations of his family have had connections with the district, but although he has a home in Leadhills he can afford to live here only part-time.

He told me why he sees the rebuilding of the railway between Leadhills and Wanlockhead as important: 'If these villages are to have a future it must be in tourism. There is no prospect of any other industry coming here. Until 1977 there was a steady slip downhill and it seems strange, but unemployment has actually helped us in that redundancy payments enabled people to buy houses because they were cheap and low-rated. Of course many of them are used only as holiday homes, but we have a community who really love living here and enjoying their leisure. It's

105

being away from it all that attracts the tourists. There's valuable business in bed-and-breakfast.'

In the garden I'd been shown the Simplex diesel locomotive and the half-dozen passenger coaches still being refurbished and regauged, not to mention 30 tons of rails and fittings and a turntable bought from Yaxham Light Railway near Norwich. As this load of rails wasn't delivered until mid-March, and timber sleepers have to be sawn to size, what the public will see at first is the half-mile leading from the site of Leadhills Station to Glengonnar mine. So far the Lowther Railway Society has spent around £9,000, and as a two-foot gauge line costs £10 per yard, they expect to spend a further £25,000 on the track by the time they get to Wanlockhead.

Alastair told me, 'We would like to see a stream of people, men, women and children, coming to these two villages that are so steeped in the history of lead mining. At Wanlockhead there is a very good museum, showing what life used to be like and the wealth of minerals that came from deep down in these hills. Visitors can go underground and along well-lit tunnels.'

The museum is in what was the engineering shop where William Symington began his experiments on steam pumps for the mines which led to the steamship *Charlotte Dundas* being launched into service on the Forth and Clyde Canal in January 1803. Symington was the pioneer inventor, and a monument to this son of Leadhills stands in the village.

Back in Woodlands Hall, I was literally on the ground floor of Leadhills's more prosperous days, for it was formerly known as the mansion house, the home of James Stirling – called the Venetian – who became mine manager in 1734 at a time when the mines were in financial straits. This nine-room house was built for him in 1733, designed by William Adam, father of the great Robert. The high, decorated ceilings, the splendid fireplaces, the elegant windows all bear the hallmark of artistic excellence.

James Stirling was 43 when he came to Leadhills, and the village was lucky to get him, for it is certain that his life would have been in the highest of ranks as a mathematician and scholar had he not had the scornful taint of Jacobite attached to him. He was called the Venetian because he had tried to uncover the secrets of the Venetian glass-makers in order to set up in competition with them.

In Leadhills he pre-dated David Dale and Robert Owen by introducing social reforms, cutting down on hours of work, drawing up rules of conduct and safety regulations, and working out a system of piece-work

Leadhills, Scotland's second-highest village. The monument is to William Symington whose pioneer steamship the Charlotte Dundas *was launched in 1803. The Lowther Hills which encircle it have been called 'God's Treasurehouse'.*

bargains with the men, whose intelligence he held in great respect. It was he who provided the Miners' Library, now known as the Allan Ramsay Memorial Library, after the poet son of a Leadhills mine manager, born in 1686. The 300th anniversary of the birth of the author of *The Gentle Shepherd* will be marked by special events in the library when visitors will be able to enjoy what is being laid out for them during the summer.

The Lowther Hills have been called 'God's Treasurehouse' because of the enormous mineral wealth taken from them since 1260 when the monks of Newbattle Abbey were mining lead in these parts. People still pan for gold here, and find it, and in the 16th century a prospector called Bevis Bulmer, with 300 men working for him, took out no less than £300,000 of gold in three summers. In more recent times miners would combine to hunt for grains of gold to make a wedding ring for one of their number about to be married.

The railway which came to Leadhills in 1901 and got to Wanlockhead a year later, proved a gold mine, too, and was said to be the best paying of the Caledonian Railway network, thanks to the heavy loads of lead it carried down the valley to Elvanfoot. Passengers were so few that the train acted as a taxi. All they had to do was wave for it to stop, or ask to be set down. It closed in 1938.

After that homely interlude with the cheery Leadhills folk I took the road south, past the Welcome Inn for the plunge down the Mennock Pass, which is closer to the Highlands in character than the Lowthers, by reason of the enclosing steepness of its hills and sharpness of descent. You come to the lushness of Nithsdale with its green fields of sheep and cattle quite suddenly, and its gentleness continues all the way down the river valley to Dumfries. What made it even more enjoyable was the soft golden light of sunset which continued all the way to the house of a friend in Dalbeattie Road where we were to be staying.

If I had just been a wee bit earlier, I might have been able to take some mellow photographs of the town, for 1986 marks the Octocentenary of the Royal and Ancient Burgh of Dumfries, which is being celebrated in a big way so that folk can appreciate the whole 800 years of development.

Sadie, the lady of the house, is a former school friend of my wife and she might not have moved to Dumfries but for our warm enthusiasm for its setting. In the three years since she came she has grown to love it, and she quickly handed me a special booklet and suggested we might spend a few hours walking the Heritage Trail.

I was a bit doubtful, for I have no stamina for walking in busy towns. What appeals to me about Dumfries is the proximity of the varied countryside stretching around it, and the Solway coast just below. But the booklet, beautifully compiled and written by Wilson Ogilvie for the Dumfries Burns Club, made me feel I would be missing something if I didn't overcome my prejudice.

So next day I did what I should have done years ago, follow the footsteps of the famous by taking the river paths and going on up to Dumfries's heights as Robert Burns, Robert the Bruce, Walter Scott, Wordsworth, Barrie, James Hogg, Mary, Queen of Scots and Bonnie Prince Charlie had done. It must have been a lot quieter for them, of course, for the modern curse of the Ancient Burgh is thundering traffic. Roll on the by-pass!

The section of the trail I liked most was along the peaceful approach by the riverside to the warm pink bridge which dates from 1430, when it replaced a wooden one built in the 13th century. Only foot traffic uses it today, and standing by the weeping willows, I looked down on a pair of grey wagtails flashing yellow as they flitted elegantly round the foot of the buttresses. Just below the level of the bridge, on the left, is the oldest house in the town, lived in until 1959 and now a museum.

In days of old, you had to pay a toll to cross the Nith on the only bridge, and more recently on the other side along what is called Whitesands, cattle and horses were sold, tinkers camped and drovers gathered. Now there is a bus terminus and you are back among the traffic. However, only a step away is the narrow Friar's Vennel, where once again you have the feeling of a quieter past as you ascend between colourfully painted shops and houses to reach the ridge on which the mediaeval Burgh eventually stood.

This is where you come face to face with a busy roundabout whose centre carries the gleaming white statue of Robert Burns in thoughtful pose, seated, hand on his breast as if wondering about the constant circling of cars and heavy lorries around him. Seen against the pink stone of Greyfriars Church with its 190-foot spire, the detail on the sensitive face is most effective.

In fact, it took a full two hours to do the round from the first bridge to the fourth because so many memories were stirred by the walk, facts of history I had forgotten. The statue of Henry Duncan, parish Minister of Ruthwell is above the Trustee Savings Bank. By chance, a few years ago at Ruthwell, I had found the little cottage at the end of the public road which became the very first penny bank in the world. Dr Duncan initiated it in 1810 at a time when public banks would not accept deposits of less than £10. He also saved Ruthwell's marvellous ancient cross.

Lack of time drove me home by St Michael's Bridge and the dock area with its bollards where sailing ships tied up when Dumfries was a busy port reached from the Solway by the Dumfries Channel. The Solway pirate, Paul Jones, began his sea career here when he became sailor boy to a Whitehaven merchant. Fighting against Britain, this boy from the village of Kirkbean was to become the greatest sea-going commander and naval strategist of his time.

Before leaving Dumfries, I drove along the Solway coast to Kirkbean hoping I'd find a museum in the house where Paul Jones had been born. Years ago, Mrs Dugan who occupies it had shown me what she called the 'Paul Jones Room', and told me it was to be taken over as a museum when another house became available for them. Sad to say, none of this has come to pass.

However, I had a look at the former shrimping village of Carsethorn which faces out to the hills of the Lake District and is always good for birds. On the sea-front you don't even have to get out of your car. Although the tide was a wee bit far out that morning, I could pick out beyond the tall forms of shelduck, a pack of scaup bobbing on the water, and on the water's edge a big pack of running dunlin, small beside redshank and oystercatchers. Pink-footed geese were flighting, too, against swirls of cloud discharging veils of rain. I took the hint and swung back to Kirkbean and headed for Kippford where a friend finds it bliss to live in a mild climate where there is rarely any snow. Over tea, he told me it takes only two hours to reach the south side of Glasgow.

Picking up my wife at Dumfries, our own way home lay over the Dalveen Pass which is the only other driving route across the Lowthers taking a parallel line east of the Mennock Pass.

AUGUST 1986

From Thornhill's wide street and grassy pavements with pollarded lime trees it is such a short trip through gentle country that you can hardly believe anything as fearsome as Crichope Linn exists in the neighbourhood. Half a mile south of the village we swung east on a minor road for the Cample Water, passing north after a railway bridge; about a mile on, we stopped at a big sandstone quarry. A wicket gate led to a well-made path along the burnside, the work of local volunteers, I learned later.

Quite suddenly we were in a different world as the walls closed round us in banks of primroses and violets. Below, a water ouzel went scurrying away, and from above came bird song from the green canopy on either side. It was like entering a canyon between red sandstone walls as our path rose to give us a grandstand view of a waterfall leaping through what was virtually a 'doorway' in the contorted rock.

Traversing rightward from the path by a slippery step, we went through the narrow portal one at a time. It made a perfectly natural place to take a cramped seat, hence the name 'Sutor's Chair'. As I stood inside the opening I saw at my hand in small, neatly-carved letters the name 'Allan Cunningham 1806'.

I tried hard to figure out what had caused this remarkably deep and narrow canyon to form. It seemed unlikely that normal flood water had done it. It is more like some of the melt-water channels I have seen, such as Rumbling Bridge near Crook of Devon where water from a glacier wore down the rocks at their weakest point. If anyone knows the scientific explanation for Crichope I'd love to hear it.

We followed a sandstone staircase of big slabs to by-pass the canyon and rejoined the path leading on, by ups and downs, to a narrow point where we could have crossed without difficulty to the other side by a mouldering footbridge. Instead we climbed to the gorge rim on the side we had been following, and once over a drystone wall, walked easily on a greensward dotted with sheep and cattle right back to where we had left the car.

On reaching home, and remembering that name – Allan Cunningham – which I had seen carved on the rock, I turned up the entry in a book where I knew I would find it, John MacTaggart's *Gallovidian Encyclopedia*. It confirmed for me that Cunningham was no ordinary chiel. He was born in the parish of Keir, Dumfriesshire, in 1784. His father was a neighbour of Burns at Ellisland and, at the age of 12, Allan followed at the Bard's funeral.

He was apprenticed to a stonemason, but showed an interest in writing from an early age.

His first published work appeared in Robert Cromek's *Remains of Nithsdale and Galloway Song* (1810). He moved to London where he became a well-known writer, contributing regularly to the *London Magazine*. He wrote novels which have been forgotten, and a play, 'Sir Marmaduke Maxwell', which was praised by his friend Sir Walter Scott, but never performed. However, he wrote the standard biography of the painter Sir David Wilkie and the monumental *Lives of Eminent British Painters, Sculptors and Architects*. He died in 1842.

MacTaggart ends his biographical piece on Cunningham with a poem of appreciation. This verse, one of eight extolling the merits of his friend, is a good example of his idiosyncratic style:

> He is na like some I cud name
>   Wha, wordy, drive alang,
> And clink away for clinking's sake
>   Not feeling what is sang.
> Mere gomerals, manufactory bards.
>   Their sangs are all a sham,
> They want the touch – the thrill –
>   the glow,
>   O Allan Cunningham!

It was MacTaggart's lively writing that decided us to drive on to Kirkcubrie which is how he prefers to spell the metropolis of the Stewartry where he had finished his schooling and loved more than any other small town he had seen in extensive travels.

It looked beautiful that afternoon as we came down the hill past a bowling green thronged with players, and on through the streets of brightly-painted houses to the Mercat Cross of 1610 and the Tolbooth where the last witch was tried and put to death in 1698. Some things have

111

not changed since this lad o' pairts, MacTaggart, wrote about it early last century. He was born in Borgue and was a self-taught engineer, writer, poet and mathematician. He had compiled his *Encyclopedia* and seen it through its printing by the time he was 34, just four years before he died. Between its publication and his death he had also written a two-volume work, *Three Years in Canada*. It was in that country he fell ill and was dead by the following year.

He had gone there to take up an engineering job for which he had been recommended by the famous bridge-builder, John Rennie, who was responsible for the bridges at Kelso and Newton Stewart, among others.

In Canada, MacTaggart helped build the Rideau Canal connecting Ottawa River with Lake Ontario, over a distance of 160 miles. The officer in charge of the project, Colonel John By, wrote of him: 'I have found him a man of strong natural abilities, well grounded in the practical part of his profession, and zealous and hard working in the field . . . a man of honour and integrity.'

We were lucky on this visit, not only to have sunshine and the freshness after rain, with big white clouds sailing, but to have a high tide hiding the expanse of muddy estuary.

In the tidal harbour I was surprised to see big modern fishing trawlers which sail as far as France, staying out for two and three days at a time, trawling for scallops which are processed here.

Standing on the bridge which spans the River Dee just north of the harbour and looking inland over the lush countryside, I was reflecting on where this water originates, thanks to the marvels of hydro-electric engineering. From Loch Doon, south of Dalmellington, it is released eastward by outlet valve and used four times through a quartet of power stations, taking advantage of the catchment of the hill country to establish a new loch at Clatteringshaws as a second reservoir with a third in Loch Ken. Built between 1931 and 1936, this harnessing of the waters has long since repaid the £3 million spent on it.

We could have stayed much longer in Kirkcudbright, but for the fact that the real reason why we were in this part of the world was to attend the wedding of a second cousin in Lochmaben, timed for noon next day, so back the road we went, this time by Dundrennan where Mary, Queen of Scots is reputed to have spent her last night in Scotland.

JAMES HOGG – GENIUS

AFTER ONE OF the mildest winters this century the sudden reversion to cold which brought snow to the hills from the Borders to the Highlands was a surprise. I wasn't complaining, because the sun was shining and St Mary's Loch was bonnier than I had ever seen it. Driving from Moffat I had stopped to climb the high path that looks into the gorge from which spouts the Grey Mare's Tail in a 200-foot fall. A pair of bearded wild goats shared the spectacular view, and from the crags came the 'kek-kek-kek' calls of a peregrine falcon.

I had been in snow up there, but standing at the Hogg Monument overlooking St Mary's Loch and Tibbie Shiel's Inn it was early summer, with peewits whooping, curlews shrilling and oystercatchers 'kleeping', while over my head went five sharp-winged birds, their burbling calls telling me they were golden plover.

As I looked from the thoughtful face of Hogg to the white square of the hostelry where Tibbie played mine host to the Ettrick Shepherd and his friends, I was thinking of the words of Professor John Wilson who shared many of these convivial nights.

Wilson, Professor of Moral Philosophy at Edinburgh University, was a writer and poet, as well as a keen angler and hard walker. He told Hogg, 'Some half-century hence your effigy will be seen on a bonnie knowe in the forest with its honest brazen face looking across St Mary's Loch.'

In fact, the monument was put up only 25 years after Hogg's death in 1835 and a huge gathering of people came to pay tribute to the literary genius who claimed less than one year's schooling in a working life which began aged seven herding sheep and teaching himself in the only university he knew – that of life.

113

The James Hogg statue overlooks St Mary's Loch, and was erected in 1835, 25 years after the Ettrick Shepherd's death. Hundreds came to pay tribute to his genius, the greatest poet next to Burns to spring from common people.

Hogg proved the truth of that couplet by Goethe:

> *Whatever you can do, or dream you*
> *can, begin it.*
> *Boldness has genius and magic in it.*

By the time the monument was erected in 1860, James Hogg was recognised by the critics as the greatest poet next to Burns to have sprung from the common people. That could be said to be accolade enough for a self-taught man who did not start to read and write until he was 18. It was when he abandoned poetry for the novel he realised his true genius, as did his contemporary, Sir Walter Scott. They were born within a year of each other, Hogg in 1770, not long before Scott, but they didn't meet until 1802 in Ettrick and immediately formed a friendship, tested by a few trials, but firm to the end.

Three miles from its emergence from St Mary's Loch, on the wall of the Gordon Arms, there is a plaque telling that it was at this inn in 1830 that Scott and Hogg met for the last time. Hogg describes the sad occasion:

> 'The last time I saw his loved and honoured face was at the little
> inn on my own farm in the autumn of 1830. He sent me word that
> he was to pass on such a day but that he was very sorry he could

not call and see Mrs Hogg and the bairns, Altrieve being so far off
the road . . . His daughter was with him but we left her at the inn
and walked down the road together till the horses were rested. He
then walked very ill indeed for his weak leg had become
completely useless, but he leaned on my shoulder all the way and
did me the honour of saying that he never leaned on a firmer or
surer shoulder. We talked of many things past, present and to come
but both his mind and memory and onward calculation appeared
to me to be much decayed. He expressed the deepest concern for
my welfare and success in life and for my worldly misfortunes . . .'

Hogg's chief misfortune was Mountbenger Farm, which he had leased
in addition to his own small farm of Altrieve Lake. Paying for it swallowed
up all the profits from his writing. The two previous tenants of
Mountbenger had failed. Hogg was soon in similar state and was forced
into selling each of his 1,000 sheep for far less than he paid for them.
Expecting to have to surrender his library, silver bowl, jug and cup, he
wrote: 'It is hard to begin a new life at 60. I am thinking of giving up
shooting and fishing and everything unsuitable to my years and
circumstances though I do not expect I can live without them.'

Luckily, though, he sat rent-free in the small farmhouse of Altrieve
Lake, thanks to the charity of the Duke of Buccleuch who had Hogg's
welfare at heart, as had the Duchess when she was alive. It was to this
little clay biggin that Hogg had brought his bride 10 years before.

He had met Margaret Philips when she was just out of finishing school
in Edinburgh, and although he had taken a great fancy to her he thought
she was far above him on the social scale – her father was a prosperous
farmer and cattle dealer.

He was 50 and she was 30 when he brought her home. Her first
surprise was to discover that the spoons were made from sheep's horns. It
must have been a crowded house, for Hogg's old father, aged 91, moved
in as well, and beds had also to be found under the roof for two maids.

By the time of Hogg's marriage he had a lot of experiences behind him.
From being a simple shepherd doing menial jobs around Ettrick, it was
the move to Blackhouse in Yarrow within easy walking distance of St
Mary's Loch which had set him on course as a young man. The farmer's
name was Laidlaw, a distant relative of Hogg's mother. The house had a
good library, and the young son Willie shared Hogg's thirst for self-
improvement.

When the young Ettrick Shepherd was out on the hill he carried a phial

115

of ink and a quill pen to copy down letters of the alphabet, put words on paper and write poems and songs. Within four years *The Scots Magazine* published him, and spurred him to further successes. The 10 years he spent at Blackhouse were happy ones and he became known locally as 'Jamie the Poeter'. It was during this time he heard a recitation of 'Tam o' Shanter', and when he learned that Robert Burns had written it, he made up his mind that if a ploughman could write like that, there was nothing to prevent a shepherd doing even better. Maybe it was then he chose 25 January as his birthday date, to be alongside Burns. (His exact date of birth was never ascertained – only the date of his baptism.)

At 31, when he was back looking after his aged parents in Ettrick, he paid for the publication of *Scottish Pastorals* which went unnoticed as do most self-published books. Then he turned his attention to the Highlands where he had done some sheep-droving. He would go north as an observant traveller and describe what he saw in a series of letters to Sir Walter Scott. The Wizard of the North was so impressed by Hogg's *Highland Tours* that he wrote to the editor of *The Scots Magazine* in 1802 suggesting these letters were worthy of publication.

The Outer Hebrides must have appealed to him, for now he thought of emigrating with his parents from Ettrick to buy a sheep farm in Harris. The deal fell through, so he became a shepherd in Nithsdale, wrote material for *The Scots Magazine*, and a book on diseases of sheep. He made money, but lost it in further unsuccessful farming ventures.

Back in Ettrick he couldn't get a job, and he made for Edinburgh to be a literary man among literary men. He launched *The Forest Minstrel* song collection, and a weekly newspaper, *The Spy*, written and edited chiefly by himself. It lasted only a year, but three years after arriving in Edinburgh he had made his mark as a writer of note.

He did it with the publication of *The Queen's Wake* in 1813. The long poem takes the form of a song competition among the bards to honour Mary, Queen of Scots. The eighth Bard's Song, 'The Witch of Fife' and 'Kilmeny', the 13th Bard's Song, lifted him into the supreme class as a poet, and Hogg, who had felt himself cold-shouldered by the Edinburgh literary establishment, suddenly found himself being invited to meet famous poets like Wordsworth, Southey, De Quincey or any other notable who happened to be in town.

Somehow I can't see a man with such a strong feeling for the countryside being happy in Edinburgh, even if he was rich. Not when he had the farmhouse of Altrieve Lake 1,000 feet above sea-level, with good hills for game rising another thousand. He had another literary success

Altrieve Lake Farm, built by Hogg after his bankruptcy. Members of the James Hogg Society sometimes come to his old home to hold readings of his works. The present farmer Walter Barrie, seen here, is very much in tune with Hogg.

behind him before he married – *The Brownie of Bodsbeck*, a stirring covenanting tale. In a letter to the author congratulating him on his marriage, Sir Walter Scott had written, '. . . to men of good temper there is no society like that of one's family.'

Hogg certainly took to marriage like a grouse to heather, and within four years had written another two remarkable novels, *The Three Perils of Women*, followed by his masterpiece, *Confessions of a Justified Sinner*, regarded today as one of the greatest Scottish novels, although in 1824 it was condemned as 'indelicate', and from it Hogg made not a penny.

However, he was making money from his other works, and by their success was led into taking the lease of adjacent Mountbenger Farm at a time when sheep farming was in the doldrums. In fact, his wife's parents had gone bankrupt, lost their farm, and were destitute, so Hogg let them occupy the Mountbenger farmhouse and moved his own family back to his wee clay biggin.

I talked to sheep-farmer Walter Barrie who occupies the house that used to be Altrieve Lake, but was later renamed Eldinhope. Walter, a member of the James Hogg Society, showed me the room where the poet died, and the study where he used to write. He told me: 'Hogg must have made some money from his books after he was bankrupt for he rebuilt the

117

house and made it into 10 rooms, with a kitchen, dairy and five cellars. He had a big household, with wife and five children, a school teacher, plus a housemaid or two.'

Hogg was also very hospitable. He wrote: 'Twenty gallons of whisky doesn't serve six weeks when the literary world is trampin aboot.' What he regretted was the waste of time when he could have been writing.

Mrs Grant of Laggan wrote:

> 'Called to see my old acquaintance, the Ettrick Shepherd, he sees more company than any gentleman in the country, not a few from England and many from Glasgow. The house is quite comfortable looking, better than you would expect, sheltered by a few tall trees and standing on a mossy pastoral – indeed – a very pretty knowe, with an extensive view, a comely crop beginning to look yellow below and the Yarrow circling round it.'

In 1832, the year Sir Walter Scott died, Hogg went to London and stayed three months, fêted by the literary crowd who knew him from *Blackwood's Magazine*, in which Hogg was featured every month in a set of intimate conversations titled 'Noctes Ambrosianæ', conversation between friends supposedly in Ambrose's Tavern in Edinburgh.

Although it was two years since Scott and Hogg had parted from each other, Sir Walter, in Italy trying to recover his health, wrote in March 1832 to his son-in-law John Gibson Lockhart about Hogg's success in London: 'I hope he will make hay while the sun shines; but he must beware that the Lion of this season becomes the Boar of the next . . . He has another chance of comfort if he will use common sense with his very considerable genius.'

What disturbed Hogg a year later was to discover that he was 14 months older than he thought, though he refused to believe his birthday was not on the same date as Robert Burns'. Two years after that, in August when he went on an annual shooting expedition, he found walking difficult, and looked down on Ettrick for the last time.

In October the doctor diagnosed jaundice, but friends recognised that he was seriously ill and feared the worst. Tibbie Shiel came over from St Mary's Loch to help with the nursing. They had known each other since they were young in Ettrick. Tibbie's verdict on Hogg was that he was 'a gey sensible man for aa the nonsense he wrote.'

To talk about her and James Hogg I went to see James Mitchell who farms Henderland just a mile up from Cappercleuch where the Megget Water comes down to St Mary's Loch. James is a great-great-grandson of

Tibbie, and has a file of correspondence that passed between these two friends. The widow of a molecatcher, Robert Richardson, who died leaving her with seven children, Tibbie turned her wee house into an inn to provide for them, and became everybody's friend. She outlived all her old customers, dying at 96, and lies buried just a few paces from the Hogg family.

What about Hogg's widow? She moved with the family to Edinburgh and the kindly Duke of Buccleuch arranged an annuity for her in lieu of the farm. Then, after 18 years of widowhood, she was granted a Civil List pension of £50 and drew it for 17 years.

The only one of Hogg's family to have children was Harriet. In 1879 she and her husband, Robert Gilkinson, emigrated to New Zealand with their nine children. Today there are reckoned to be a hundred descendants of that family in New Zealand and Australia.

I was delighted to hear that members of the James Hogg Society sometimes come to his old home to hold readings of his works and to talk about the remarkable character who once lived there. It is good to know that he is not forgotten but very much alive in local lore.

AROUND SCOTT LAND

S IR WALTER SCOTT declared that from the top of his beloved Eildons he could point out 40 places famous in Border history and ballad. In lieu of his profound local knowledge I had with me Keith Robeson, Countryside Ranger based in St Boswells, to identify the features of the vast landscape that lay before us in sunshine and shadow.

Northward he pointed out green Lauderdale, the snow-sprinkled Lammermuirs, and away beyond the cluster of Galashiels, the wintry Moorfoots; westward I could identify the Three Brethren cairns pinpointing the Minchmuir, and in memory follow the old drove road to Traquair and on to the Tweedsmuir hills and St Mary's Loch. Now the landscape was fitting together.

Across the Tweed stood Dryburgh Abbey and on the same line, but slightly left, the pinnacle of Smailholm Tower jutting from a rock edge and only 10 miles from the English border. The curve of the blue Cheviots – no snow on them – signified the Debatable Lands of bloodshed and feuding.

But for watering eyes in the bitter wind, it would have been a pleasure to walk around this summit ringed by the Iron Age fortifications inside which there were once as many as 300 dwellings. Out of the wind, though, we could chat comfortably, as Keith pointed out where the Romans had their camp just below Newstead above a curve of the Tweed. A short traverse over the heather and below us was Melrose and its Abbey containing the heart of Robert The Bruce, it is said. Just up the Leader Water, another hill-top fort on the 1,000-foot crown of Black Hill, beyond which lay the village of Earlston, erstwhile home of Thomas The Rhymer.

In this country of oral tradition and ballads handed down over the centuries, it is hard to sort out fact from fiction. On the road just below our hill, there is a slab you might take for an old-fashioned direction post.

What it carries is an inscription telling that it is the site of the Eildon Tree, where Thomas The Rhymer met the Queen of the Fairies and was carried off on her white horse to Elfland where he remained for seven years. In Elfland he was gifted with a tongue that would never lie, and the ability to foretell the future.

On the day before Alexander III was thrown from his horse at Kinghorn in a thunderstorm, Thomas The Rhymer had forecast that there would be a wind that would blow a great calamity and trouble for Scotland. It was the death of the king, and the English Edward I consequently trying to enforce his will on Scotland, that led to the Wars of Independence, which were to destroy so much and leave in ruins the priceless Border abbeys of Melrose, Dryburgh, Kelso and Jedburgh.

Robert The Bruce gave money for the restoration of Melrose, where he intended his heart to lie, but subsequent destruction and the Reformation took their toll. In Walter Scott's time it was being plundered for its building stone, until he persuaded the owner, the Duke of Buccleuch, to put a stop to it.

It was that other abbey just across the Tweed, Dryburgh, which in this century drew attention to the predictions of Thomas The Rhymer, especially the one:

> 'Tide, 'tide, what'er betide,
> There'll aye be Haigs of Bemersyde.

The Press took up the story of Thomas when Field Marshal Earl Haig, commander of the Western Front in the First World War, was interred at Dryburgh in 1928.

On the Tweed nearby, the Haigs held land in the 12th century, and a 16th century tower formed part of a later mansion, altered and enlarged in the 17th and 18th centuries. When the Haig lands were alienated from them in the 19th century, it looked as if Thomas The Rhymer's prediction was false. Not so, however – for his services to the nation the Field Marshal was granted Bemersyde. The simple headstone over his grave is that of a common soldier, and round the corner from it is the grave of Sir Walter Scott.

Scott's *Minstrelsy of the Scottish Border* has the magical ballad of Thomas The Rhymer in it, but what do we really know of True Thomas? In their authoritative *A Dictionary of Scottish History*, Donaldson and Morpeth say: 'Mentioned in charter 1260–1270, evidently wrote *Romance of St Tristram*; his reputation as a prophet was referred to from the 14th century onwards; alleged to have spent seven years in Elfland.'

Some say that Elfland was, in fact, Aberdeenshire, and that Thomas's disappearance was timely, since he got out of the way of Edward's army by going into exile in the north-east. I visited Earlston to look at the ruins of the Tower which was his home, and to see the plaque that tells of his final disappearance when, after a night of feasting with friends, he went out and was never seen again.

Eildon and Leaderfoot, with Melrose as its centre, is one of the 40 areas of outstanding scenic significance which must be conserved as part of our heritage, say the Countryside Commission for Scotland. Kelso is well outside this area, but as a town I think it is the most attractive in the Borders.

Sir Walter Scott had some of his early schooling here, and regarded it in his maturity as having the air of a French town, with its spacious market square, its ancient abbey and great chateau, with a parkland setting where the north-flowing Teviot joins the Tweed.

I was standing in the square listening to the sweet chiming of the town clock striking 12 when a burly man with a Rotarian badge in his lapel came over and said how pleased he was to see me. I told him I was interested in the Scott connection with Kelso, since I knew he went to school here, lived with his Aunt Janet, and became friendly with the Ballantyne brothers with whom he was subsequently in partnership.

'Come with me,' he said. 'I'll introduce you to a man who knows more about Kelso than anybody else in this town.' He took me across to his watchmaker's shop, and within minutes I was shaking hands with local historian Dr J. Trainer.

Off we went immediately for a stroll, which took us round the abbey and across the car-park, where in front of us, was a detached house with a cast of Sir Walter Scott on it. My guide told me it was a wee cottage with a thatched roof when Scott's Aunt Janet lived in it. A top storey was added last century and it is now called Waverley Cottage.

Steering me round the corner along a narrow street, he pointed to a shop front marked 'Hairdresser'. 'That was where Scott's first book was printed, the *Minstrelsy of the Scottish Border*. The press of James Ballantyne and Company was there. This firm, with Constable as publishers and booksellers, were to become his partners in profit and bankruptcy.'

Saying goodbye to Dr Trainer, author of *Kelso, Yesterday, Today, Tomorrow*, a short walk took me to the house where John Ballantyne had lived in style. Today it is a listed building occupied by two Border artists, Mr and Mrs McDonald Scott, who welcomed me to Walton Hall and talked about the pleasure of living and working by the Tweed.

I'd written about their work before, though I'd never met them. Both are painters, but it is Anne who is an interpreter of the Border ballads and creates lovely little models from wire dressed in clothes of the period. The tiny lifelike dolls are placed on little stages illustrating, for example, the rescue of Kinmont Willie from Carlisle Jail; the Queen's Four Marys; Thomas The Rhymer meeting the Queen of the Fairies; or the Lament for the Border Widow. The place to see them superbly exhibited is Smailholm Tower, five miles west of Kelso.

By the time Scott's *Border Ballads* were published, he was Sheriff of Selkirkshire, had explored parts of the Borders, where few tourists ever went, and been disappointed in love. However, within a remarkably short time he met and married a lady of French extraction, Margaret Charpentier and set up house at 39 Castle Street, Edinburgh.

It was when he moved nearer to Selkirk and became tenant of the farm and manor of Ashiesteel, taken on lease from a soldier cousin serving in India, that the writer in him was released.

For Scott the past was always present. A favourite short outing from Ashiesteel was to Elibank, a gaunt ruined castle set high above the Tweed, once the home of Sir Gideon Murray who had an ugly daughter known as Muckle-moo'd Meg. In this castle dungeon, an ancestor of Scott's had a difficult decision to make. Young Wat of Harden had been caught lifting Murray's cattle. He was given the choice of being strung up and hanged, or of marrying Meg of the Muckle Moo. Marry her he did and they were very happy.

Scott would have bought Ashiesteel if he could, but with the lease running out in 1812 he moved with his pigs, calves, sheep, dogs and ponies to a farm beside a filthy duckpond, known locally as the Clarty Hole. He gave it the name Abbotsford, because the land had belonged to the Abbot of Melrose in former times.

With him went Tom Purdie, his shepherd, whom Scott had first encountered when Tom was up before him on a poaching charge. Scott was so taken by his plea that grouse were plentiful and work scarce that he eventually made him farm manager at Abbotsford.

It was when the Scott family – husband, wife, Sophia (13), Walter (11), Anne (9), and Charles (7) – were squeezed into the small farmhouse by the duckpond that Walter resumed work on his novel, based on first-hand accounts of men who had survived the Jacobite Rising, following the Prince to the disaster of Culloden. Scott had listened to tales from the lips of some of these brave men, and heard many stories from other sources of people who remembered the last vicious war

This fine portrait of Sir Walter Scott hangs in the private sitting room of Mrs Patricia Maxwell Scott at Abbotsford.

to be fought on Scottish soil and the terrorism which followed the defeat of the Highland Army.

Waverley was not only Scott's first novel, but the world's first historical novel. A mystery, though, is why he didn't declare himself as author. Was it because he had a financial stake as partner in its printing and publishing firm, Ballantyne and Constable? Or was it the fear that novel-writing might be thought to be too frivolous an occupation for one in the legal profession?

Waverley was only the first of 32 novels by 'The Great Unknown', who was to be gazetted Baronet in 1818, the same year as *Heart of Midlothian* was published. By this time, such was his popularity across the Atlantic that watchers on Beacon Hill, Boston, scanned the sea for a sail bearing the latest book.

It was to the famous house which Scott created from his profits – Abbotsford – I went next to renew acquaintance with Mrs Patricia Maxwell Scott, great-great-great-granddaughter of Sir Walter, and to have the privilege of a private visit to its inner sanctum which, in summer, is a place of pilgrimage for thousands of all nationalities.

Everybody was welcome in Abbotsford, it seems, when Sir Walter was alive, with 2,000 acres of well-managed estate. His hospitality was

I was given a rare privilege in Abbotsford, to sit at Scott's desk and to hold the quill pen he used. When I tried the master's spectacles, I found they suited my eyes to perfection.

proverbial. After his death the world kept coming as it still does. The story is well-known of how this most successful writer in the world, and one of its most-loved men, was suddenly reduced in circumstances when the firm in which he was partner went bankrupt. As its only earner, he set himself the task of paying off a debt of over £100,000. He had always been a fast writer and in the six years remaining to him he worked himself into the grave.

In the famous study, I asked if I might be allowed to sit at Scott's desk in his leather chair, and hold his white-feathered quill pen in my hand. I was offered his spectacles as well, and found they were as clear for reading as my own. For light he had gas, made on the premises from oil. His bedroom was just above the study, and he was always first down in the morning, the coal fire set, ready for a match when he began writing.

He was 61, and worn-out from writing works well below his usual standard, when he looked out on his beloved Tweed for the last time on the golden autumn morning of 21 September 1832. In these half-dozen years of declining health he had paid off £80,000. 'When he died and his mind was affected, he thought he had cleared it all. I'm so glad of that,' said Patricia. The books, in fact, brought in the remainder of the money after he was laid to rest in Dryburgh Abbey.

This is how James Hogg sums up Sir Walter Scott:

'What are kings or emperors compared with Sir Walter Scott? Dust and sand. He is a man that next to William Shakespeare will descend with rapt admiration to all ages of futurity.

'Is it not a proud boast for an old shepherd that he could call this man friend, and could associate with him every day and every hour that he chose?

'Let Abbotsford be secured for his lineal descendants, as nothing can be effected to preserve the remembrance of one whose name and fame are immortal.

'Blessed be his memory. He was a great and good man.'

No one has ever been able to refute that last statement. The public have been faithful to Scott. The entry money they pay preserves the baronial mansion and its historic contents as Sir Walter knew them. Long may they keep coming.

FROM SUMMITS TO THE SEA

THE KINGDOM OF FIFE and the Royal Burgh of Kilrenny, Anstruther Easter and Anstruther Wester straggles from hill to shore and faces out to the Isle of May. In the past I've tended to think of Anstruther as a holiday resort for golfers, caravaners and touring motorists. I didn't realise it was an architectural gem with history round every corner.

The local folk call it Enster and they make a clear separation between Easter and Wester, even though the Dreel Burn that separates them has long been bridged and the two communities are now one. Before 1630, however, to get from one to the other meant crossing the burn on stepping stones. That was the way James V walked, bagpipes under his arm, disguised as a travelling player so that he could enjoy his dominion un-noticed. A sharp-eyed beggar woman is said to have recognised the Royal visage as he was about to get his feet wet, the stepping stones being under water. She stepped in, lowered her shoulder for him to hang on, and, kilting her skirts, carried him over.

Today's stepping stones are much closer to the sea than in James V's time. The new set is made of concrete blocks for the convenience of folk who would otherwise have to detour to the bridge. I chose to go over them, passing great sea-walls and the enormously thick sandstone ones of an ancient castle whose tower was once 60 ft. high. Sir William Anstruther lived in it at a time when English, Dutch, Danes and French fishers were invading the Forth. He didn't accept their presence and would go out with his men to drive them off, thus earning the nickname of 'Fisher Willie'.

From Anstruther, it is open water for 400 miles all the way to The Netherlands, something which was to prove very convenient in later years

Picturesque Anstruther no longer hosts great fleets of fishing boats, but its old world character draws tourists to the East Neuk of Fife.

for smuggling wines, spirits, tobacco and Dutch cloth into the village. The red-pantiled roofs of the fresh-washed buildings are relics of the time when these tiles came over as ballast in Dutch ships that sailed back home with coal and linen. Just round the corner of the Dreel Burn is the Smugglers Inn, and even the manse of the old kirk had a secret passage to its garden.

In the 16th century kirkyard there is a stone coffin that was supposed to have floated over from the Isle of May bearing the martyred body of St Adrian. It is actually the remains of an old burial kist, and was probably brought here when there was an older kirk on this site. The spire of the present parish kirk – now used as a hall – was too good a landmark in its time. Cromwell's army desecrated it, using the kirkyard as a stable and tossing the pulpit bible into the sea when they sacked the town.

It is said the Dreel Burn was handy for body-snatchers who could sail up from the old harbour, carry out their business and make off in their boat.

The prosperous period in Anstruther's history came in 1883 with the herring boom when up to 9,000 barrels were coopered in a day by 76 tradesmen, and the long harbour front was noisy with the shouts of men

Easter in Glen Torridon, and the huge bulk of rocky Liathach rises about its reflection in Loch Clair. In geological terms, the glen is said to be the oldest in the world, its bed rock Lewisian gneiss, with layers of Torridonian sandstone, topped by Cambrian quartzite.

The noblest scenery makes the poorest agriculture. Highland cattle and crofting fields at the head of Loch Torridon, and above the abrupt rise of Liathach.

Frost mist covers Loch Lomond; left in the middle distance are the highest trees on Incailloch – the Island of the Old Women – with snowy Ben Lomond rising above.

Ptarmigan, the mountain grouse, whose summer plumage matches the rocks and lichen. In winter it changes to white to match the snow, and in spring assumes another plumage. Internationally it is known by its Gaelic name, and is the hardiest of all arctic and mountain birds.

Lambing time in the Lowther Hills. The scene is the Dalveen Pass at over 1,000 ft. between the Rivers Nith and Clyde. A shepherd scatters food pellets to his flock on a chilly April evening.

Smailholm Tower, the splendid Border keep above Sandyknowe Farm where Walter Scott lived with his grandparents and an aunt who inspired the imagination of the future author with stirring Border tales.

The Border mansion of Abbotsford built by Sir Walter Scott to overlook the River Tweed. It is still home to his descendants, and its historic contents are open to the public.

No hills in Scotland are more sensitive to the play of light and the movement of clouds than the Cuillin of Skye. In this photograph, on the left is the main ridge known as the Black Cuillin, and on the right the Red Cuillin.

From Laig Bay on the Isle of Eigg, looking to the Cuillin of Rum, as filtering rays make gold of the sea.

Tammie Norrie, the Sea Parrot, the Puffin, call it by whichever name you choose, it is the most entertaining to watch, and Scotland holds about 700,000 pairs, that is 90 per cent of the British and Irish breeding population. These three were on a Shetland headland.

Razorbills. The Outer Hebrides and Northern Isles, Sutherland and Caithness hold more than 75 per cent of the Scottish population of this seabird, pictured here in May on the Barra Head.

Yacht skipper Graham Tiso on the cliffs of Barra Head. In wild weather fish are sometimes thrown up to land on top of the 600 ft. cliffs.

The eastern entrance to Glen Lyon where the narrow road threads above the deep-cut river. October is the time to see it like this.

Remnant Caledonian pines frame the eastern view of Glen Lyon above Meggernie Castle. West of this the glen becomes barer. Passes lead north to Rannoch and south to Loch Tay. The driving road ends at Loch Lyon.

and women, gutting and curing, and a constant coming and going of boats. Apart from 3,500 fishermen and boys, nearly as many as half that number were connected with the industry.

I wondered why there was so little stir in and around the harbour today. I talked to Tom McBain, an official of the Scottish Fishermen's Federation.

'No fish sales take place here now,' he told me. 'Pittenweem's where the boats go to sell their fish, as its deeper water is more suitable for landing the catches. A hundred years ago this harbour had no equal for fishing in Scotland, but now it is hardly used. The focus of fishing has moved north to congested Peterhead. Our harbour needs modernisation for the bigger boats used today.'

Thanks to the Anstruther Improvements Association you can learn a lot as you walk around. A plaque on a house tells you it was the home of Captain Keay who held the clipper-ship record, when with the wind in his favour he managed 340 nautical miles in one day on the run from Hong Kong to Gravesend. His ship the *Ariel* did it in 83 days, beating the *Teiping*, captained by Captain McKinnon of Cellardyke. Always there was rivalry between these adjacent fishing towns. Even at school, boys fought each other, a Cellardyke man of my own age told me.

As dusk fell, I drove down to Pittenweem, and what a stir of activity there was about the harbour, the lights of tied-up boats dancing in the water, as some moved out and others came in. Fishermen I met were in fine fettle, shouting across to each other. In the fish-houses, folk were busy, some loading vans to go off selling round the villages. I ordered a box of lemon sole, just off the boat to be ready filleted for the morning, and I've never tasted better.

MAY 1987

Just as I was about to leave the East Neuk of Fife I had a request from the recently-formed Save the Wemyss Ancient Caves Society, whose conservation aim is to preserve from vandalism what remains of the priceless Viking and Pictish drawings, said to be in greater concentration within these caves than elsewhere in Britain. One drawing of a ship is said to be the oldest known in these islands.

The Society is hoping to place obstacles at the mouth of the caves to prevent cars being dumped and set alight to the destruction of the drawings by early dwellers incised when the sea-level was higher.

Macduff Castle marks the site of the Wemyss caves that contain Pictish incised drawings, urgently requiring protection.

With the request to publicise their work came an informative booklet entitled *The Wemyss Caves* written by Frank Rankin. The name Wemyss is from the Gaelic, Uamh, meaning cave. These haunts of Picts, Norsemen and smugglers have suffered in recent times through misuse, wilful damage and neglect.

The caves were easy enough to find. All I had to do was look for the ancient tower of Macduff Castle on the seaward side of the cemetery and make my way by a marked path.

Two wee boys were lighting a fire just inside the mouth of one of the red sandstone caverns when I walked along. They knew about the drawings and pointed out Jonathan's Cave, named after a man and his family who lived in it at one time. I was told that inside could be seen drawings of a ship and a fish.

The cave proved to be no mere opening, but a huge vault going back 50 ft. with a bench-bed at the back and seats cut into the west wall. I soon found the famous ship, once my eyes became accustomed to the gloom, and among modern graffiti I could discern where sharp tools have pecked out horse, dog, fish, elephant, goose and deer symbols I'd seen on Pictish stones elsewhere in Scotland.

Coal-mining has caused collapses in some of the caves. In 1934 brick supports were built by the Wemyss Coal Company to prevent the loss of the Court Cave, but another subsidence in 1970 makes it dangerous to enter now. In this big cave the Baron Courts used to be held, hence the name.

The sinking of the Michael Pit and mining of its seams caused the Glass Cave to collapse. It contained one of the earliest glassworks in Scotland, operating from 1610 to the 18th century. The Well Cave had a passage that led into Macduff Castle, but unstable ground has made this cave dangerous too.

Alas, in 1990 vandalism is still rampant, and even a padlocked steel gate fixed over the entrance to Jonathan's Cave failed to stop the vandals. After three padlocks had been ripped off, a mortice lock was substituted. Not only was this burst open, but the gate itself also was stolen and the culprits turned their attention to removing steel bars of the grille.

In 1989 large boulders and concrete blocks were dumped to act as a sea-wall to combat the constant erosion that is steadily eating away the coastal front of Jonathan's Cave. There is a problem of money, and a feasibility study has stressed the importance of the Wemyss caves and Macduff Castle as a common thread in the tourist plan, with a visitors' centre, lecture facilities, shop and restaurant.

Possible sources of finance for regeneration would include local authorities and national agencies such as the Scottish Development Agency, Tourist Board and European funding. The Save the Wemyss Ancient Caves Society is still striving to influence these bodies to act before it is too late.

LARGO REMEMBERS SELKIRK

THE FOLK WHO have the good luck to live in the auld Seatoun o
Largo declare their village to be the Riviera of Fife's East Neuk.
Take that as a bit of local bias if you like, but I can tell you it felt like it in
the few days I spent there recently. My guide was Allan Jardine,* a
descendant of Alexander Selkirk's brother, so the first stop had to be the
famous statue erected by Allan's grandfather David Gillies, 100 years ago.

We approached it by way of a narrow street of traditional cottages. The
life-size statue looks down from the second storey of one of these and the
plaque reads:

> In memory of Alexander Selkirk, Mariner, the original of
> Robinson Crusoe, who lived on the Island of Juan Fernandez in
> complete solitude for four years and four months. He died 1723.
> Lieutenant of *HMS Weymouth*. This statue is erected by David
> Gillies, net manufacturer, on the site of the cottage where Selkirk
> was born.

It shows a rugged, bearded figure dressed in goat-skins, sewn into
knee-length trousers and tunic, his right hand shading his eyes, the left
gripping his gun. It was the work of T. Stuart Burnett, and was cast in
bronze at Leith by Sir John Steele, R.A. When the Countess of Aberdeen
unveiled the statue on 11 December 1885, 500 railway excursionists
travelled from Dundee to witness the ceremony.

Allan Jardine's wife, Ivy, has researched the life of Alexander Selkirk,
even travelling to Chile and flying from Santiago over the Pacific for 2½
hours to make a dramatic landing on the island where Selkirk watched
every day for a ship to take him off. She went with her son, Allan, and two

* Allan Jardine Snr. passed away not long after this was written.

The famous statue of Alexander Selkirk in Lower Largo. Its plaque reads: 'In memory of Alexander Selkirk, the original of Robinson Crusoe, who lived on the Island of Juan Fernandez in complete solitude for four years and four months. He died in 1723, Lieutenant of HMS Weymouth.'

friends from Largo to meet the people who live on the island which has been re-named Isla Robinson Crusoe.

She looks back on the trip as a wonderful adventure, and recalled for me the thrill of dropping out of the clouds on to the island's tiny airstrip perched sensationally on the edge of 800-foot sea cliffs. Waiting for them were fishermen with mules to take them and their luggage down arid slopes to the seashore, and into a fishing boat for a thrilling two-hour sail to the inhabited part of the island. On the way, they passed sea-lions basking on the rocks and admired the changing colours of the water, alive with fish. As they sailed, two lobsters were cooking over a fire in the centre of the boat. These were later served to the passengers along with the local white wine.

The islanders came out to greet them with shouts of welcome and the first thing Ivy did was plant the heather she had brought beside the Crusoe Hotel. Ahead of them were six days of exploring the 12 by 5 mile island, including a climb up to 2,800 feet to the look-out point which Selkirk visited every day in the hope of seeing a sail. Once he had to run for his life when pursued by crew from enemy ships, and only his fleetness of foot saved him.

Up there, Ivy's son, Allan, placed a commemorative plaque with the words:

Plaque placed here by Allan T. Jardine, direct descendant of Alexander Selkirk's brother, David.

REMEMBRANCE
Til a' the seas gang dry
and the rocks melt wi' the sun.

The plaque is beside another placed there by Commodore Powell and the officers of *HMS Topase* in 1868. It records that Alexander Selkirk '. . . was landed from the *Cinque Ports* Galley, 96 tons, 16 guns, A.A. 1704, and was taken off in the *Duke*, Privateer, 12th February, 1709.'

A privateer is a ship owned and officered by private persons authorised to capture merchant vessels. The *Cinque Ports*, on which Selkirk was navigator, was such a ship. He asked to be put ashore because of the leaky state of the vessel. As a result of gun-battles it was in a dangerous condition, and the death of the Captain had placed in command an officer he disliked intensely. Selkirk had pleaded that the ship should dock for repair. This was refused, so he demanded to be put ashore on Juan Fernandez with his belongings and some food.

He knew that there was water and firewood on the island, that there were goats and sea-lions and turtles, and that he could survive as other people had done, notably an Indian, marooned by accident, who had spent three years there before being rescued. English sailors had also been marooned there in the late 17th century. It was well-known as a good anchorage for buccaneers.

What Selkirk didn't know, though, was how he would cope with loneliness, for his life had been spent on crowded ships where living space was at a premium. He was 28, and soon became depressed and melancholy. At first, he lived in a cave and ate only when he was driven by hunger. Later, he moved into the hills where he built two huts. Rats nibbled his bare feet, so he made friends with cats descended from domestic animals which had abandoned ships for a life ashore.

He might have settled down more happily to island life if he had known that the *Cinque Ports* had foundered shortly after he left, and that the eight who survived were taken prisoner by Spaniards and held in a Lima jail for seven years – among them the hated Captain. As it was, it took him eight months to find contentment in solitude. Reading, praying, and singing psalms had brought comfort and ease of mind. In later life, he claimed his Christianity had been a great comfort to him.

The Largo party were taken to Selkirk's cave, and found two families living in it and some women outside cooking, as children played nearby. They saw the wild goats whose flesh and hairy skins had been lifesavers for Selkirk. The islanders live mainly by fishing, and there is an abundance of wild vegetables and fruits. Without cars, newspapers and television they lead a simple life and entertained their visitors with flutes and guitars.

They had never seen or heard the bagpipes. Allan, who had been pipe-major at Fettes College, put that right by playing them selections and two

Mrs Ivy Jardine and her husband Allan stand on the site where Selkirk was born. It was thatch roofed; demolished in 1862, it was replaced by the house with the red door shown. Mrs Jardine and her son Allan visited the island. Allan is a direct descendant of Alexander Selkirk's brother David.

special pieces: one a lament in memory of the period of melancholy during Selkirk's first year of loneliness, then a reel as the navigator found joy in his desert island life.

The modern history of the island is tied up with the Falklands. When Britain claimed them from illegal possession by Spain in the 18th century, the Chilean Government installed a garrison on Juan Fernandez in case of a take-over by Britain. About 120 years ago, the island became a penal settlement. The islanders today are mostly descended from these prisoners.

Since returning home, Ivy Jardine has never been able to forget the beautiful island and its tranquil way of life. She would love to go back and spend at least a year there and do something for the people, perhaps teach traditional Scottish dancing, Fair Isle knitting and handicrafts. However, she has been putting her time to good use at home, researching the history of Largo and working on a second volume to complement her privately published *Seatoun of Largo*, a collection of Victorian photographs.

Under a picture of the fishing harbour as it used to be, she has these words:

> 'He that will view the Kingdom of Fife must go round the coast, and no coast in all Great Britain has so many quaint, charming old sea-side towns with histories so interesting.'

The quotation is from Daniel Defoe (1660–1731) who was a political agent as well as a prolific author. He was deeply interested in promoting British trade with the South Seas, and there is no doubt that he was intrigued by the rescue of Alexander Selkirk by the ships *Duke* and *Duchess*.

Finding Selkirk was a stroke of luck for Captain Woodes Rogers, for

135

about 50 of his men were in a bad way with scurvy and required fresh food and vegetables to cure them. They were taken ashore to camp and a party went with Selkirk to collect all the food they needed. He amazed them by outrunning the ship's bulldog to catch a goat. He knew where succulent greens grew, and the sick men were soon on the mend.

When it came to leaving the island, his knowledge of local winds and currents was of immense value.

Within a short time he was given command of a ship with a crew of 100 that had been taken as a prize, and he was to go halfway round the world before returning home with £800 in his pocket, his share of the loot. It was a voyage with plenty of risks, raiding along the Pacific coast from Chile to Panama, dominions of Spain at that time. The most rewarding booty was gold and silver being taken from Mexico and Peru to the Spanish Treasury in Europe.

Rich in plunder as the voyage was, it was high on hardship, in ships holed by gunfire, with much fever and dysentery on board. In hungry times men ate rats and paid as much as sixpence for them. It was October 1711 when Selkirk arrived back in England via the Hebrides. The full story of the first circumnavigation of the world for 123 years can be read in *A Cruising Voyage Round the World* by Captain Woodes Rogers.

It doesn't tell, though, of the return home to Largo by Selkirk, arrayed in splendid finery, when he was thought to be long dead. Even his mother didn't recognise him for it appears that his face had become much more thoughtful looking. Indeed, it was remembered by his shipmates privateering with Woodes Rogers that he was never rough with captives, but kindly, especially with the women.

Happiness, however, he seems to have left behind on the island, for he is quoted as saying, 'I am now worth £800, but shall never be so happy as when I was not worth a farthing.'

He was restless and couldn't settle to an idle life. Sometimes he would take a boat to Kincraig Point and stay there for a time because it reminded him of his island. He took solitary walks, a favourite one being to a ravine known as Keil's Den where a burn ran close beside the ruin of an ancient keep.

It was hereabouts he met a 16-year-old girl milking a cow. Her name was Sophie Bruce and he ran off with her to London. About a year later we hear of him going to sea as a naval lieutenant. Before his departure he made a will consigning all his worldly goods to Sophie.

In 1719, he was aboard *HMS Enterprise* in Loch Alsh in a flotilla of three frigates intent on bombarding Eilean Donan Castle, then occupied

Lower Largo harbour with the Crusoe Hotel centre. The village lays claim to be the Riviera of the East Neuk of Fife.

by a force of Jacobites reinforced by 300 Spaniards. The castle was reduced to ruins, and a land battle between Government forces and the Jacobites took place in Glen Shiel, the defeated Jacobites retreating over the top of a Kintail peak now known by the name of Sgurr nan Spainteach – the Peak of the Spaniards.

When next we hear of Alexander Selkirk, he is in Plymouth, married to a merry widow by the name of Frances Candice who kept a public house much frequented by sailors. On his wedding day, he made a new will leaving all his worldly goods to his wife, then he went to sea, contracted fever, and was buried at sea somewhere off the coast of West Africa. In Largo, the date of his death under his statue is 1723. It should be 1721.

Some time later Sophie Bruce wrote to a vicar telling him that two of her uncles were Church of Scotland ministers, and that she was destitute. She contested the claim of Alexander's widow to his effects, but because of differences between Scottish and English law, she lost.

As for Alexander, maybe he was easy prey for a scheming woman who worked fast. One thing is certain: the enterprising navigator spoke the truth when on his return from Juan Fernandez he said he was a better man in his solitude than ever he was before, and feared he would ever be again. He triumphed over adversity, and the island that bears the name Isla Robinson Crusoe is his true memorial.

SKYE IS HARD TO BEAT

IT WAS THE morning after he had flown the Atlantic and driven himself from Prestwick to Skye that I renewed my acquaintance with Rob Parker, International Director of the Clan Donald Trust. We met in the superbly-converted stables which now form the reception area and restaurant of the Clan Donald Centre at Armadale. Rob had spent a week at the Annual General Meeting of Clan Donald USA, where 300 members from as far afield as California, Florida and Atlanta had gathered.

I didn't know very much about Rob, except that he is a Scot, with a Scottish wife, who had held a high executive position in the States before giving it up to exchange a desk in Manhattan for one in Armadale – a risky move, I thought at the time. He agreed, and explained why he and his lively wife, who helps in running the Centre, took the big step into a new life.

'I'll give you my background. At 23 I was studying accountancy. I'd just done my National Service, and decided to emigrate in 1959. I started work with Eastern Airlines, and in time became the manager of La Guardia Airport, the second biggest in its system. I'd a staff of 575 when I moved after eight years to become manager of Kennedy Airport. I'd been moved up to Sales and Marketing when I left on a two-year contract to come here.

'The Clan Donald Trust had asked me to consider coming back to Scotland to run their Centre. They invited me to see over the place before giving them an answer. That was in 1978. I spent four days looking around the derelict buildings and the 40 acres of the surrounding policies. My first impression was of disappointment. I felt that any clansman coming here from abroad would have the same feeling.'

The Clan Donald Centre at Armadale on the Isle of Skye. Opened in 1978, its purpose is to appeal to an estimated 3,000,000 MacDonalds scattered all over the world, and it has proved a magnet for visitors.

I have written earlier in *The Scots Magazine* that this was my own impression when I had looked at the ruinous stables, the run-down farm without a cattle-beast, and the overgrown driveways telling a story of neglect and dereliction. Speaking to a cross-section of local folk, I had not been able to find one native Skyeman who thought the Clan Donald Trust would make any difference to the general run-down at Armadale. The folk of Sleat looked for salvation to the merchant banker Mr Iain Noble who had bought 20,000 acres of MacDonald land and inspired a whole lot of new projects, including the Gaelic College.

Rob continued, 'I felt there was only one way for the Clan Donald Centre to go and that was UP. Theirs was a big challenge here, and a chance for me to do something for Scotland and Skye. I've always been interested in history and genealogy. Money isn't everything. Here was a non-profit-making organisation. At half the salary I was earning, I decided to give it two years, and go back to the USA if it didn't work out. I've burned my boats now and have no regrets. This is the garden of Skye – there's no other place like it for variety of trees and vegetation. We'll take a wee walk to some of the paths we've made to outstanding viewpoints.'

139

I was impressed by the thought which had gone into these. International Volunteers and the Conservation Corps had worked hard clearing the vegetation so that paths could be laid to little low-walled bays, each with an indicator plaque explaining the view and detailing the clan history of the various areas.

Visiting overgrown parts round the high walls of the ruined laundry, Rob told me of his plans to restore it and turn it into a piping school. I liked the feeling of parkland which now shows off the noble trees such as monkey-puzzle, redwoods, huge spruces and other exotics. Paths lead through natural woodlands and the most popular walk takes about an hour. Countryside Ranger Duncan MacInnes is on hand to help and explain wildlife to visitors.

While I was waiting for Rob to arrive from the airport, I had taken the chance to visit the restored part of Armadale Castle, to look at 'The Headship of the Gael' exhibition, the Clan Donald Museum and take a seat in the little cinema to see the audio-visual programme telling the story of the Lordship of the Isles.

Rob was keen to hear my impression, for much thought by prominent Gaels had been expended on where the emphasis should lie.

In the end, they had come up with 'The Sea Kingdom', the period of around 400 years when Clan Donald was strong and negotiated politically with England, Ireland, France and Scotland. At its peak their rule extended from Kintyre to Assynt in Sutherland. Beginning with Somerled, the 12th century progenitor of the Clan Donald, through to his successors into the 15th century, when James IV broke Clan Donald power, this was the longest period of peace and prosperity the Highlands and Islands had known.

The aftermath was clan against clan without the rule of law. At the end they were fighting to protect their way of life.

I told Rob I thought it was a masterly presentation, and mercifully not romanticised. 'The Headship of the Gael' exhibition can be taken at leisure, each section in its own little compartment as you wind through a crypt which takes you from pre-history to the present, via the Clearances.

Armadale Castle is not ancient despite its empty shell. The second Lord MacDonald built it in the early 19th century when there was a large revenue from kelp. Lived in by some of the family until the 1920s, it was then let out with shooting in pre-war days. What Rob hopes for within the next 10 years is a partial restoration with five floors in use. On the ground floor he would like to see a gathering room for several hundred and above it Australian, Canadian and United States of America floors, each telling its own story of Gaeldom. The top storey could be devoted to the Clan Donald Trust.

His main consideration is to get the place used. This year has been the best yet with 60,000 visitors. The Centre has been a great boost to the hotel and bed-and-breakfast trade and the actual construction work has helped local businesses. The very high primary school roll of 66 speaks for itself. Young folk who might otherwise have left are staying in Sleat.

In its beginning the Macdonald Centre had only one full-time employee. In 1990 it had 45 in summer and 19 in winter. It now houses one of the most important collections of Highland historical material in a new Library, Exhibition and Study Centre. Its 6,000 volumes are open to researchers, and include the Macdonald Estate papers, maps, prints and genealogical records.

In 1990 the Sir John McDonald Study Fund was announced, awarding a sum up to £10,000 annually for research to further the understanding of Highland culture.

I was present in the Raeburn Room of Edinburgh University when Ian McDonald, Chairman of the Clan Donald Trust, presented the first award from the Fund to a gently smiling William Gillies, Professor of Celtic Studies, to enable him to take a year-long sabbatical and delve into the history of Clan Donald from the 10th to the 18th centuries. From the Gaelic manuscripts known as the Red and the Black Books of Clanranald, the Professor is working to produce a scholarly account in one volume.

Rob Parker considers that the native islanders are the main asset of the Clan Donald lands. If there are no good job prospects they will move out and be replaced by incomers, which is not the same thing. Said Rob with feeling 'I want to see Sleat conserving the West Highlanders by offering something that everybody who comes will enjoy. It is happening.'

I spoke to local folk about this, and they agreed that the Trust has turned out to be a very good thing despite their early pessimism. Sleat is undoubtedly the community with the healthiest growth in the Highlands and Islands.

How does the Clan Donald Trust organisation work? It has a Board of Trustees, nine from the USA, four from the UK, one from Canada and one from Australia. They meet in Skye once a year. There is also an Executive Committee which assembles in Skye three times a year and comprises Mr Ellice McDonald Jnr. – Chairman; Lord MacDonald, a hotelkeeper from just up the road; Clanranald; and Douglas MacDonald, a Scot working in Switzerland. To date, £2½ million has been spent by the Clan Donald Trust, and Rob pays high tribute to the help given by the

141

Highlands and Islands Development Board, The Countryside Commission for Scotland, the Nature Conservancy Council, The National Heritage Fund, and The Museum Trust.

By far the major financial contribution has come from the charitable organisation the Glen Coe Foundation, whose total amounts to £1,600,000. This charity is named after a Glen Coe MacDonald who emigrated to Canada and became a powerful figure in the Hudson Bay Company. Ellice McDonald Jnr., its administrator, is a descendant with a deep interest in Scotland.

I asked what would happen if the Trust died a natural death. I was shown the answer in the Trust Deed of the Clan Donald Lands Trust, registered on 20 April 1971. The relevant portion read '. . . the whole assets shall be offered to the National Trust for Scotland for its purposes.' In Rob I believe they have a Director who can create projects, lay them out and submit them in a workable form that will get results. He has the will and the energy.

Although I've been coming to Skye for 50 years, it is only in the last two decades that I've been trying to get to know the great variety that lies outwith the orbit of the magical Cuillin.

With my wife, I took the chance to see a new bit thanks to choosing Buel-na-Mara, a bed-and-breakfast house in Broadford. We made friends with its two young proprietors, Paul and Grace Yoxon, who opened it in the spring of 1984 as a Field Centre. They'd done some hectic joinery, decoration, plumbing and painting to get it ready, for the first courses had been arranged for 16 March.

Grace and Paul are geologists who met at university in England, and came to Skye with a field expedition. They loved it so much, that when they returned for a holiday in 1980, they knew that the Misty Isle was the place where they would like to live. Grace read an advert for a secretary in the police station at Broadford, applied, got it and liked it.

Paul, then working on the oil rigs, based in Aberdeen, became a commuter after the pair got married in 1981. Their home was a rented croft in Lower Breakish, and during two years there their thoughts were centred on prospects of work at a field centre proposed for Broadford, but which never came off. There was a baby on the way, and Paul's work for a geological consultancy firm forced them to move and buy a house in Crieff. However, they found finance to take them back to Skye, bought the Broadford house and moved in on 23 December 1984.

These were some of the things we discovered about the happy pair with

Paul Yoxton who with his wife runs the Skye Environmental Centre at Broadford. He is seen here with rock fossil ammonites which he found at a headland of Suishnish.

the good-natured toddler, before we went to bed. In the morning it was planned that Paul would show us one of his own discoveries, the headland of Suishnish lying due south of Torrin where he had found on a cliff of Jurassic rock fossil molluscs dating back 19,000,000 years. He had already shown me a 70 lb grey rock with an unmistakable starfish outlined on it. He had carried it up from the area of Loch Leatham below the Storr, the first reasonably complete starfish fossil found in Skye.

The rough track to Suishnish is the ancient route to a large crofting settlement, and on its ups and downs I was delighted to come across two stonechats, my first sighting for a long time of what used to be a common bird. The approach was over rust-coloured moor grass, then almost suddenly we were into greenery and the ruins of crofts abandoned in the mid-19th century.

It is the old story of compulsory clearance. In 1853, those who refused to emigrate to Australia or move to another part of the estate were removed by MacDonald's factor and the houses burned. Among the very old who clung to their homes was a woman of 96. Ordered out, she spent several weeks without a roof over her head. That January, they evicted cottars from their shelter, the evictor being the Inspector of the Poor acting for the Trustees and Lord MacDonald. This period of clan history is remembered, too, in the Clan Donald Trust Museum, and rightly so.

Parking the car at a sheep fank and house still with a roof, a short walk took us to the shore and a cave where rock doves flew out, but there was no sign of the otter which Paul has seen a few times here. I was thrilled by the fossil cliff and the inset whorls of ammonites. We had an exciting traverse rising high to avoid cliffs where a waterfall spouted, and then it was up over the top of Carn Dearg to descend by Loch an Leoid back to the car.

It is the immense variety of Skye which appeals to Paul and Grace. Their dream has proved to have the magic they envisaged. They have found the Skye people much more friendly than those in their native England, and find the young folk polite. Their Field Centre now has the status of 'Skye Environmental Centre' and a varied range of holiday courses are on offer.

From the lounge window, I watched turnstones and curlews foraging for food, and out on the water, eiders, mallard and shags. A day or two before, there had been a great northern diver.

If, like me, you love all aspects of Nature, Skye is hard to beat.

The Voyage of The
Sea Eagle

A S A YACHTING skipper, Graham Tiso is a man of few words. His duplicated note to Iain Smart and myself was terse. 'We'll pick you up on Saturday at Ullapool pier. Personal kit and sleeping bag are all you need. I'll attend to the food. You bring liquid refreshment.'

Early as I was, Iain had beaten me to it, and we promptly set off to a position behind the village and looked to Ben More Coigach and the entrance to Loch Broom to see if Tiso was going to be on time. 'That must be it,' said Iain. The binoculars showed a white, streamlined yacht with tall masts, sending a bow wave under engine power over the flat calm water. It was too distant to read her name, but soon we knew it was Tiso's brand new vessel as it swept nearer and turned into harbour to tie up beside a fishing boat convenient for handing our stuff to the fourth crew member, David Stone, who'd helped to sail the boat north from Southampton, where it was built.

This was to be the yacht's first long voyage in Hebridean waters, and I had asked for a difficult target, North Rona, 45 miles north-north-east of the Butt of Lewis and notoriously difficult to land on by reason of its cliffs exposed to Atlantic surf. Within minutes of going aboard we were turning towards the sea and taking stock of a vessel incorporating many features resulting from Tiso's 10 years of adventurous sailing. I thought his old boat the Fifer ketch *Mysie* had everything, but, as Graham said, 'It doesn't compare with *Sea Eagle*. We've had a marvellous sail, she's a tremendous sea-boat, really comfortable in heavy weather in the way the *Mysie* was not. I'm delighted with the way she responds to the lightest airs. You know there's 11,000 lb. of ballast in this boat!'

We looked with admiration at the teak decks on a fibreglass hull, and at the masts 55 ft. over our heads. With Bermudan rig, the ketch not only

145

Sea Eagle *sets sail from Ullapool en route for North Rona. Teak-decked on a fibreglass hull, with a mast of 55 ft. and a Bermudan rig, the ketch has auto-pilot, echo-sounder, log, radar, radio telephone and satellite navigation.*

Crew members (left to right): Iain Smart, David Stone and owner Graham Tiso, mountaineers all.

The pinnacle known as the Old Man of Stoer on the north coast offers a challenging climb – if you can cross to it.

looks a thoroughbred, but is equipped with auto-pilot, echo-sounder, log, radar, radio telephone and satellite navigation.

Achiltibuie and the Summer Isles were just ahead of us now, and south behind us a welter of summits were emerging rightward from the rocky serrations of An Teallach, to A' Mhaighdean, Slioch and the Torridons. What I was looking forward to was the sight of Suilven and the Assynt peaks, not to mention the Old Man of Stoer, a miniature Old Man of Hoy. David had once climbed it, and he made a wry face as he remembered being suspended on the climbing rope between pinnacle and mainland with the waves dousing him as he fought his way over.

Round the other side of Stoer Point we had the grey quartzite ridges of Foinaven in view, fronted by the sharp peak of Ben Stack and the bare hulk of Arkle, with the island of Handa as a possible landing prospect. But now the weather was roughening, and it was starting to rain, so we nosed under the famous bird stack instead, enjoying its verticality and the marvellous natural sound box the canyon made for the yelling of birds, chiefly kittiwakes and guillemots.

In the souring weather, we began to think of the best anchorage for the night, and Graham switched on the radar to find the entrance to Loch Laxford and follow in deeply to perfect shelter near its head. We had sailed 42 miles from Ullapool and were ready for the fine meal that

147

Graham immediately set about preparing. The time was 7 p.m. and in the 13 hours since leaving home, I felt I had had a surfeit of twisting and turning on road and sea, so it was good to enjoy the absolute quietness.

The cooking arrangements and internal layout of the saloon of this 'Sea-farer' yacht are splendid. Sitting at the dining-room table you have a view of the outside world, and with two stainless steel sinks and an immersion heater you are never short of hot water for washing up or having a shower. Soon we were tucking into homemade soup and pork chops and all the trimmings, with fruit to follow. Graham did all the work, for he enjoys cooking and takes a pride in it.

I was delighted that I had found my sea legs so quickly in what had been not exactly a calm passage. My bunk in the bow was bliss, and I slept like a baby until awakened by the anchor chain rattling over my head as it was hauled up. It was 7 a.m. as we started moving and Graham brought me tea in bed. 'It's wet. Stay in for a bit,' he advised. I dozed, gradually becoming aware that the boat was rolling and tossing, that my throat was dry, and that I was beginning to feel unwell. My sea-sickness tablets were handy. I swallowed two, but didn't manage to hold them down for long.

I knew how rough the sea was the moment my feet hit the floor, but I made it to the toilet, doing my best not to knock myself out as I retched like a fulmar. A few bouts of this, and Graham came to the rescue. 'Take my bunk at the after end. I should have thought of you in there. It's the worst place in a sea like this. You'll be all right back there. Just lie still.' I did, and didn't have to get up until I heard a cry at 2.30 p.m. of, 'Land-ho. North Rona!' What I saw was a black hump above a swirl of sea and drifting mist. Seven hours of dead reckoning had brought us to this first glimpse of it.

Warily, Graham engined closer, watching and taking echo-soundings, for the chart is not very specific here about hidden rocks. With the wind in the north, our landing would have to be on the precipitous south coast about which Frank Fraser Darling had written in *Island Years*: 'Once in a blue moon a man may jump ashore on the south coast of the island and then climb a hundred feet of bare rock to get on to the green.'

A careful traverse of the mile-long cliffs turned us round to look again at a deep cut slicing like a prow into the cliff and marked on the chart as Poll Thothaton. Blue moon or not, it was our only hope. Running the anchor down and fixing an additional 56 lb. lob weight to the chain for extra holding, Iain and I were soon ready to try a landing with David at the oars, and Graham staying with the yacht meantime.

On the swell, the tiny dinghy felt like an eggshell. Judging his moment

North Rona, the most north-westerly point of the Outer Hebrides, and a major breeding ground of Atlantic seals. Landing was difficult that day of high breaking waves.

carefully as the craft rose and fell close to the rocks, David said, 'The decision is yours now. Step off when you see the moment.' We did, each in turn, on to hornblende gneiss, sound rock, but steep, very slippery and demanding the greatest care. By the time David got back to the boat, Graham had decided that it was safe to leave the yacht unattended. The tricky part of their landing was hauling the dinghy to a position where it couldn't be swept away, leaving us marooned.

All now on the island, and mighty pleased with ourselves, we climbed rapidly to its crest of greensward, loud with protesting blackbacked gulls, whose eggs we carefully avoided. What I was looking forward to was arriving at the edge where the cliffs fall over, to see the untold thousands of puffins Darling had described so vividly. He had said the two species were interdependent, the greater blackbacks arriving when the puffins came to nest, and leaving again when the puffins went back to sea. He had described the cliffs as being littered with the skins of puffins pulled neatly inside-out, the technique used by blackbacks.

I was greatly disappointed to find hardly any puffins, nor was there the show of seapinks which Darling believed was due to the draining effect caused by puffins digging holes and fertilising the soil by their droppings. We saw plenty of old puffin burrows, but only a hundred or so of the quaint red-nebs. Fulmars had taken over where the puffins used to be. Nor were there any arctic terns on the island's only beach on the Fianuis. Another change from Darling's time is an automatic lighthouse and helicopter pad, built in the late 1970s.

The lighthouse stands on the Tor at 355 ft. on the eastern side, the highest point of the island, and looks down the narrow headland of low-lying ground, the most northerly point of the Outer Hebrides, often impassable in wind-driven spray and undercut by tunnel caves reaching far under the headland. It was on the narrowest neck of the Fianuis that Darling erected his two wooden huts for a six-month stay into winter, battening them down with cables and raising walls with stones for extra security from the wind. He and his wife never really felt safe in the terrible storms because the sea on both sides was so close. Yet the huts were still there when they returned the following year in 1939.

Rona takes its name from Ron, the Gaelic for seal, and when the Celtic ascetic set up his cell in the 8th century, he took Ronan for his name. The Fianuis is the only low part of the island where seals can haul ashore, have their pups and mate with the bulls in the wild months from autumn to winter.

The Darlings grew to love the life of this place. After enduring for months everything that the Atlantic storms could throw at them, he writes:

> 'I could do fine to become a modern Ronan and live there the seasons through for a few years more, watching the birds come and go and pass through, and the great seals populate the place in the wild autumns. Oh, Rona, Rona!'

That cry from the heart remained with him into old age. He cherished the experience more than any other of his marvellous island years. Even his face reflected the loving memory of it as he spoke with me shortly before his death.

That was why I was so keen to come here, to see where he lived above a natural tunnel where the boom of the sea was terrifying in storms. That Tunnel Cave was just as he described it, running in from the Sgeildige Geo, with two branches which were virtual cellars under the floor of the hut. Not only could they hear the whisper of the moving water in calm, but also the falsetto cries of the seals in wonderful harmony – magnified in this echo chamber.

From the Tunnel Cave we climbed a thrilling edge of rock to look at the cliff of the Geodha Blatha Mor, of vertical yellow pegmatite in contrast to the grey gneiss, a place yelling with kittiwakes, and air busy with fulmar petrels following every quiver of updraught on stiff wings, large dark eyes sometimes meeting ours at a few yards' range, with a 300-foot drop between.

A short grassy walk from here, and we were on the ups and downs of cultivation rigs with St Ronan's cell and the ruins of the village where five families once lived. When the geologist J. MacCulloch landed on Rona in 1818, he found only one man in occupation, paying a rent of eight bolls of barley and eight stone of feathers for the privilege. And just in case he might desert before his term was out, he was not allowed a boat.

After him arrived a shepherd from Lewis who left in 1844, followed, after a gap of 40 years, by two shepherds from Ness, who came in May 1884 and died the following February. I'd like to know more about this pair and what caused them to die at the same time. The reason they came to Rona, it appears, is because they quarrelled with the parish minister of Ness on Lewis. We have to turn to the scholarly Martin Martin, and his *Description of the Western Isles of Scotland* to find out anything about the earlier inhabitants of the village. His source of information was Daniel Morison, minister of Barvas parish which includes Rona, who had visited the island in 1680 and recounted it to Martin 15 years later.

At that time, the population was five families who grew barley and oats and had cattle and sheep. Their greeting to the minister was, 'God save you, pilgrim, you are heartily welcome here; for we have had repeated apparitions of your person amongst us, and we heartily congratulate your arrival in this our remote country.' The minister was not so pleased, however, when one of them walked around him sunwise, a pagan custom. At each house, the occupants saluted him, took his hand and said, 'Traveller, you are welcome here.' For him each householder killed a sheep, whose skins were filled with barley meal. That was his 'present'.

Soon after this, the entire population died of hunger. A plague of rats from a wreck ate up their stores, and a passing ship, looking for fresh meat, stole their bull. They were discovered by the steward of St Kilda, who found a woman with a child at breast, both dead, by the side of a rock. The rats, it seemed, also starved when all the food was gone. A fresh colony of islanders was established by the minister, but of them perhaps the only remaining signs are the deep-trenched cultivation rigs. In time

151

the island was offered to the Government as a penal settlement by Sir John Matheson. The prisoners today are 200 sheep from Ness.

Fraser Darling was excited by the chapel of St Ronan who, it is recorded, came from Eoropie in northern Lewis. Today the chapel's occupants are fulmar petrels, one of them inside the fireplace beside some of the artefacts which Darling had discovered during his excavations. The drystones of the chapel are laid as for the black houses of Lewis, as Darling says 'in direct descent from the culture of the Megalithic Age.' Wisely, in such a notoriously windy island, family houses seem to have been mostly underground, with only the thatch showing. Lacking peat, fires would have been of turf.

North Rona has been a National Nature Reserve since 1956, and scientists carrying on the good work of Fraser Darling have a strong hut, secured and shuttered, incongruous beside the ancient chapel. For them this remote island is within Sea King helicopter distance with no need to stay long on what, for Darling and his wife, was truly a desert island. That was the romance of it for them, the only sign of civilisation being the stones going back 12 centuries and the cultivation rigs of those who knew only the old way of life, hardly changed from primitive times.

It was three days before Christmas on a clear, calm winter day after snow when they sighted the cruiser that would take them back to civilisation, a rose-tinted morning when the two of them went to the chapel for the last time. He wrote: 'We may never see Rona again as we saw it that morning early; no one else alive has been there at such a time, but we felt in these quiet moments that our farewell was not forever.'

Mist was beginning to obscure the island and the air felt raw and cold as we jogged down the steep slope from the chapel to the cliff, where the dinghy was secured. We descended with great care, knowing the serious consequences of a slip. Once back at the yacht we set off for another island associated with the men of Ness, Sula Sgeir, where each year an adventurous party lands and stays to take a haul of gugas, solan geese fat from the nests.

It was 10 p.m. when we drew close to this jagged spine of rock dotted with cairns like stone men. The automatic lighthouse flashed its beam, seals bobbed on the water and birds fluttered from below our bows.

I fell asleep to the creaking of the sheets to awake in Loch Carloway, not far from Callanish Stones.

After breakfast we discussed our next target, the Flannan Isles.

*   *   *

JANUARY 1985

There was something I did not appreciate when the three of us landed on North Rona. It was that we had gone ashore precisely within 100 years and one day of the arrival of the last human settlers to die there, the two shepherds of Ness in Lewis who had chosen voluntary exile on this uninhabited island remoter than St Kilda.

We reached North Rona on 21 May 1984 – the shepherds arrived on 20 May 1884. It was the wording of the tombstone which made me decide to follow up their story and try to determine the cause of their deaths within seven months of their arrival there:

SACRED TO THE MEMORY OF
MALCOLM MCDONALD NESS
WHO DIED AT RONA
FEB 18 1885, AGED 67,
ALSO M. MCKAY
WHO DIED AT RONA
SAME TIME

Blessed are the dead
who die in the Lord.

Looking for clues, I turned to a modern history, *Lewis* by the late Donald MacDonald, published in 1978. Part of the story was there, but naturalist J. A. Harvie Brown who had visited North Rona in June 1885 gave a much more detailed account in a lecture delivered to the Royal Physical Society.

It seems the two shepherds left Ness because they felt guilty for objecting to the appointment to their kirk of a lay preacher. To atone for their sins, they went into voluntary exile on North Rona, setting up house in the old settlement near the chapel ruins. They were visited by men of Ness in August and September, but could not be prevailed upon to return. They seemed to be happy, repairing sheep fanks, fishing and killing seals that came ashore to breed.

They were enterprising men, and there was no reason for anxiety on their behalf until an old lady of Ness by the name of Flora Macdonald began to have premonitions of evil so strong that she walked 15 miles to friends of the exiled men to urge them to set sail to the island. The Ness men succeeded in landing on 22 April at the third attempt. Feelings of foreboding struck when nobody appeared to meet them.

In the passageway leading to their semi-underground house they saw Malcolm McDonald sitting as if asleep at an improvised fireplace bearing a cooking pot. He was dead, as was his companion who lay inside the house wrapped in a plaid. The Ness men assumed death to have been from natural causes and they wrapped the bodies in canvas sheeting and buried them in the graveyard by the chapel wall. Back home, however, perhaps because of the premonitions of the old lady, rumours of foul play began circulating. Questions were raised in Parliament. Eventually, the Stornoway Fiscal was ordered to carry out an investigation, and he set off with two medical men, two coffins, and a son of one of the dead, to carry out a post-mortem examination. They found death to have been from natural causes. Murdoch McKay had acute inflammation of the right lung and left kidney. Malcolm McDonald, who had nursed him, had died of cold, exposure and exhaustion. It is thought that he was in the passage because he did not wish to stay in the room with the dead body.

It seems they had spent much of their time in prayer and reading Gaelic scriptures. For calculating the weeks they had cut notches in a piece of dressed wood, one for each day and a deep one for the Sabbath. The notches ceased on 17 February, the very day when Flora Macdonald began to 'see' something evil had happened to the men out on that lonely island. A strange story indeed.

Sea Eagle Sails On

ONE OF THE pleasures of arriving at a new anchorage in the dark is awakening in the morning to an entirely new vista of sea and islands. After our adventures on North Rona and a blissfully long sleep, there was no feeling of hurry to leave Loch Carloway on Lewis for our next destination – the Flannans. Not when there was fun to be had exploring a complication of islands and narrow channels between them.

Graham, our skipper, pointed out on the chart how very narrow the channel is between Little Bernera and Great Bernera, with skerries scattered beyond them in an area called Poll Gainmhich. Once through the exciting passageway, we were in our element, with the heads of Atlantic seals bobbing around us, guillemots and razorbills scuttering out of the way, gannets diving, and rock pinnacles hewn with natural arches changing shape as we swung about.

Turning south we came through the Kyles of Pabbay past the crofting township of Valtos, dimmed by rain and heavy skies. Suddenly Graham gave a loud shout, pointing up at a large bird soaring in and out of the cloud over the island hump of Vuia Mor.

I could see it was no golden eagle. This bird had longer and squarer-cut wings and the tail was short and rounded. I could not see the flash of white that would have confirmed the matter, but I had no doubt that it was a sea eagle, one of quite a number released from Rum in the past few years in the hope that they would live long enough to mature and raise a new generation for Scotland.

Since Graham's boat is named *Sea Eagle* I shouted that it was a good omen as I handed over the binoculars, but with the movement of the boat and the obscuring clouds he was unable to pick it up. However, we swung in to land on the island over which it had flown – Buya Moir it was called

155

by Dean Munro in 1549 when he described it as '. . . mair nor ane myle lange, inhabit and manurit, full of natureal pasture for store, fishing, and excellent guid fewall. It pertains to McCloyd of the Lewis'.

The word 'fewall' refers to peat and on top of Vuia Mor there was plenty of it, and just above where we landed, the rigs of former cultivation. The green crown of the island rising to 221 feet was in contrast to its rock-banded coast, giving us some excellent scrambling and leading to a marshy lochan where twites were twittering and a wren singing. Just off this point, too, was a fishing boat hauling its creels, a visitor, for nobody lives on Vuia Mor now.

That night we anchored in a quiet land-locked corner of Floday Island. By 7 a.m. we were off again, all three sails set for the Flannans, and since visibility was almost nil in the drizzle, I stayed in my bunk for the 20-mile cruise to these 'Seven Hunters', the largest of which was our immediate target, the one bearing the lighthouse whose three keepers mysteriously disappeared in 1900 shortly after it was built. Today the light is automatic and Eilean More still holds the secret of the missing men. Those who came to investigate the cause of the light going out saw an open door, a table spread for dinner, a chair overturned on the floor, but no evidence of what had happened to the men.

Centuries before there were such things as lighthouses, the MacLeods of Lewis used to land to hunt the wild sheep, possibly of the St Kilda variety and brought to these islands by Norsemen who probably put them there for food during their western forays. Even before the Norsemen came raiding, Christian followers of the Celtic church had built a chapel to commemorate St Flannan on the crown of the island near where the lighthouse was sited.

Remembering these things, we drew close with anticipation, but it was something of a surprise to see how precarious the landing was going to be – by an iron ladder on the vertical rock face. First we had to find the fixed buoy for mooring. Then, with the dinghy launched on a heavy swell, and David at the oars, Iain and I got in and were soon nosing in to the deep cleft marked on the chart as Skiobageo and watching for the moment to grab a rung of the rusted ladder, to start climbing. Without the ladder, landing would have been impossible in the heavy swell.

Once up, we found ourselves on a platform from which sprang a wall of cliff bearing what was once a long zig-zag of steps concreted on to the face, with an iron handrail to help balance. Weather and time had twisted off the rails and a central section of the staircase had collapsed. Crossing that gap was more akin to rock climbing.

On the largest of the Flannan Isles, where three lighthouse keepers disappeared in 1900. The island still holds the mystery of the missing men.

The situation was thrilling despite its artificiality. Looking directly down into the sea, we could see pale shapes of seals swimming, and everywhere was a crying of birds echoing out of a cave right below us. We marvelled at the ingenuity of the lighthouse builders who had provided a walkway to the very crown of the island.

In fact the concrete pavement leading all the way to the lighthouse had also been the base for a light tramway hauling supplies from an airy crane position situated vertically above the West Landing with a branch line to the East Landing.

We had to wait until we were on top before we saw the tall light tower rising 75 feet, its beam powered today by a long-lasting supply of acetylene gas, and monitored from the Butt of Lewis lighthouse. There was little to see through the creeping grey mist, and since all doors to the building were firmly locked there was nothing to inspect. Wanting to stay on the summit crest, we had to set off along the west cliff-edge. The way led to two ancient drystone bothies beyond which we were once more on the brink of a void.

Then a black wedge of pinnacle solidified level with our eyes like a prow cleaving the moving mist, and suddenly its precipice stood revealed from summit to sea, with a glimpse of slunging channel between us and the sharp peak. We were looking at the skerry shown on the chart as 'The Sgarr' and its ridge facing us had a snow of seabirds right to the summit, mainly guillemots, fulmars and razorbills. Our own island had shaken off its mist, too, and looking back we saw its summit quilt of greenery crowned by the white stock of the lighthouse making us feel it was a friendlier place than we'd thought.

Retracing our steps, I took a close look at the tiny chapel dedicated to St Flannan who had set up his cell at a slightly lower level than the lighthouse. As I examined its neat construction, I wondered just how many Leach's petrels were brooding single eggs amongst its stones. It has been said that the Flannans belong to these little slate-grey, tube-nosed birds which fly in from the ocean at darkness to take over from their sitting mates. The fork-tailed Leach's petrels are the rarest of our nesting seabirds, and are found on only a few of our oceanic islands.

Alas, we couldn't wait for dark and their return if we were to sail to the other islands of the Flannan group, but we did have time to explore Skiobageo, a deep creek penetrating like a tunnel into the crags near where our dinghy was hauled above the West Landing. David and I were first to go in, entering under a great cathedral arch of vaulted roof echoing with the shrieks of kittiwakes. The chamber became ever narrower and darker and we were almost hypnotised by the rise and fall of the boat on the swell. In the confined space the slunging sounds were magnified to an almost frightening extent.

We had passed Atlantic seals asleep on ledges above us on the way in, no doubt deposited there at high tide. In our minds was the possibility that one of them might overturn us in such a narrow channel if it became alarmed. In its rush to escape it might well hit the dinghy. Unlikely, perhaps, but all the same we felt it better to turn back towards the distant daylight.

At the time of the disappearance of the lighthouse-keepers, Lewismen who knew Eilean More gave their opinion that Skiobageo might hold the key to the mystery. They had seen mighty waves burst into the blind tunnel to explode back outwards and rush in a wall of water up the rock face of the West Landing. The official explanation, by a Mr Robert Reid, is not so specific. 'I am of the opinion that the most likely explanation of the disappearance of the men is that they had all gone down on the afternoon of Saturday, 15 December to the proximity of the West Landing, to secure the box with the mooring ropes etc., and that a large body of water going up higher than they were and coming down upon them swept them away with resistless force.'

Common guillemots crowd a Hebridean nesting ledge on the Shiant Islands.

Two events confirm that the accident happened on 15 December 1900. The skipper of the *Archer* noted that the lighthouse wasn't shining on that stormy night, and the last entry in the lighthouse log was for 9 a.m. on 15 December. Bad weather delayed the relief vessel, and it was Boxing Day before the *Hesperus* arrived.

Before hauling the dinghy aboard the *Sea Eagle*, we made a reconnaissance of the deep and narrow inlet called Geodh an Truillich, but judged the heavy swell too dangerous for landing on neighbouring Eilean Tighe. Instead we sped off for Roareim, the most westerly rock stacks of the Flannans. They were a delightful surprise in every way, with a gannetry which I didn't even know existed.

Everything here was exciting: the seals following our boat, the bulls lying on rocks, so confiding that they merely raised their heads to watch us pass, and guillemots, razorbills, shags, and puffins in droves scattering out of our path. Every skerry was of bare, clean gneiss, veined with yellow branches of pegmatite, a few with natural arches.

With sails set for Lewis, we passed Soray and Sgeir Toman, the southernmost of 'The Seven Hunters', well pleased with how the day was turning out, with soft sunshine as we came under the rock-speckled gneiss of the Harris hills turning between two impressive buttresses to anchor in Loch Tamanavey for a good feast and comfortable sleep.

Morning mist was clearing to soft sunshine when we upped anchor for a fast sail to Toe Head with our cruising chute spread and billowing like a spinnaker. We watched the big hills of the Clisham group and the island of Taransay slip past, and entered the Sound of Harris. Because of its shallows and marker buoys, it requires careful navigation, so we took in the sails and motored past Leverburgh and Rodel, then north-east to reach Loch Bhalamuis just north of Scalpay at sunset.

It would have been grand to have been on the Flannans that glorious day of vivid sea colours and bright greens, but these thoughts were banished in the morning when we hoisted sail for the Shiant Islands and in an hour and a half were going ashore on the beach between Garbh Eilean and Eilean an Tighe. We had a feeling we were arriving home, for Iain and I camped here for a week a good few years ago, and had also landed more recently in fine weather.

We hardly expected third time lucky on these marvellous bird islands, but this was the most vivid yet, the lichen on the huge columnar basalt rock pillars even more orange than we remembered, and sprays of white and pink campion hanging with purple vetch and yellow buttercups. The birds on Garbh Eilean are not so much on the cliffs as on the tremendous boulderfields of collapsed rock columns. Shags, puffins, guillemots and razorbills erupted from below our feet as we picked our way along. I have never seen such a density of shags on land and sea.

The highlight of our visit this time was being able to land on Eilean Mhuire, the island of the Shiants on which we had never set foot. Smaller than the two main islands, its distant greenery belied its precipitous nature when we got close. Even the landing was steep, and its eastern tip a real surprise, a narrow ridge soaring to a pinnacle with a ferocious drop into the sea. The criss-crossing fulmar petrels below gave us a sense of vertigo.

Yet everywhere on its lush green top were signs of former cultivation, more than you might expect to support the ten families who occupied the two main islands until the end of the last century. We could have sat long enough enjoying the sun and the whirling cloud of puffins going round and round in front of us, but it was time to be sailing again, for Iain and I were due in Ullapool the following morning, and David and Graham had to start work on Monday, which gave them just a day and a half to sail on for Oban.

With the wind still holding north, and the hills of Harris and Skye falling astern, we all agreed it had been a great sailing holiday in the best place in the world for it.

Sea Eagle Has Landed

IT WAS BLISS to get out of the choppy sea on which we had been pitching and rolling for five and a half hours, and sail into the comparative shelter of the low-lying Monach Isles, west of North Uist. Eriskay had been our anchorage the night before, and I had decided against breakfast in the Sound of Barra, guessing what it would be like in the open Atlantic with the strong wind against us. Unfortunately my fears of sea-sickness had been justified.

As the anchor went down and I crawled up on deck, Dave, the first mate, remarked on how quickly I had risen from the dead, when skipper Graham Tiso passed me a mug of tea and a cheese sandwich. My climbing pal, Iain Smart, the third member of our crew, was acting as second mate, while I was happy to be described as a landsman who obeys orders when able.

This was the same quartet who sailed the *Sea Eagle* to North Rona and the Flannans on her maiden voyage last year. Since then the yacht has covered over 5,000 nautical miles, from the outermost Hebrides to the Scilly Isles. For Graham, however, there is nowhere like the Hebrides – he loves isolation and the challenges of difficult landings.

Now that we were here we could hardly wait to get ashore, encouraged by the sight of numerous birds skimming the water. On the sea and over our heads were twisting packs of chattering turnstones and cleeping oystercatchers; little terns, smallest and most buoyant of the sea-swallows, circled above, and eiders and shelducks below us were ringed by the bobbing heads of curious seals. We certainly didn't have far to row ashore, for only a short distance away was the abandoned lighthouse of Shillay, perched on rocks where over 2,000 Atlantic seal pups are born every autumn.

161

When this lonely tower was working, there was a saying among mariners: 'If you see Monach light, you're too near.' It operated for 78 years, and there is a story of a gale in November 1881 wrecking two attending boats. One December, a shaft broke and the light-keepers kept the machine turning by hand for 17 consecutive nights; cold and strenuous work, for which they were commended for 'special zeal and activity'.

We climbed to the top of this red-brick lighthouse – a dark and dusty ascent, until we came to the big prisms on their mountings weighing two and a half tons – the part the zealous keepers had turned by hand. From the top we saw how little divided us from the crashing Atlantic waves – no more than low reefs. Our boat rocked gently at anchor between them and the open sea.

Back to the boat for tea and a lump of cake, after which we rowed to the next island, Ceann Iar, meaning West Head. Landing was easy, and just above where we hauled the dinghy was a row of mounds with stones at head and feet and a little cairn with this inscription:

Lieut. R.N.R.
W.A.McNeill
HMS Laurentic
25 Jan. 1917.

The graves are below the ruins of an old township, now occupied by fulmar petrels and starlings. If any reader knows the story of the mishap which caused the death of these men I would be interested to hear it.

Birds were everywhere: a tight pack of sanderlings with some turnstones and dunlin on the white sands of the sea-edge; eider ducks and drakes, with shelducks, in the tussocky grass; blackheaded gulls and terns made a lot of noise; a buzzard was being shooed off by oystercatchers; meadow pipits and rock pipits and skylarks rose from our feet; snipe were in the air.

Returning against the waves was tricky for Graham and Dave, and with some misgivings, Iain and I watched the tiny dinghy disappear in the trough of the swell. They took so long to reach the boat that Iain reckoned they would lift anchor and pick us up at the far side of the island. However, we saw Dave cast off, and through binoculars noted he was wearing a life-jacket. We were grateful that he carried two for us.

Dave and Graham are expert at managing a dinghy in difficult places, not getting too close to avoid being dashed against the rocks, but nipping in on the retreating wave. Then it's up to the boarding party to judge the moment to jump. It worked perfectly, but not without drenching our feet and trousers. Without the life-jackets I would have been really worried. A tiny dinghy in a sea like that can't be anything else but menacing.

Once we were safely back on the yacht, Graham decided to move to a position closer beside two lobster boats which had come in for shelter, and moored nearer inshore. Glad to have less movement, we were soon tucking into a real throat-burner of a peppery stew with mash which needed a cold drink to cool the thrapple and neutralise the heat. Then to bed.

In my bunk in the foc'sle I slept well, until wakened by the slosh of water and crash of dishes rolling about. Then I heard Dave's calm voice. 'Graham, we seem to be aground and leaning to starboard.' It was only then I realised I was in the angle between my bunk and the curve of the bow. It wasn't uncomfortable, and since the two experts didn't seem worried, neither was I. By daylight we were fully afloat and on an even keel. Graham and Dave had known we would come to no harm on the seaweed-covered bottom.

On rising from his bunk Graham sprang into action before breakfast, sure that *Sea Eagle* was dragging anchor and getting too close to the nearest fishing boat. By moving to shallower water for shelter, the cause of our dragging now was due to having less anchor-chain out. Anxiety mounted, however, when, as he tried to lift the anchor, it hooked on a ground-chain. For a moment or two it looked as if we must strike the fishing boat, but quick thinking and good seamanship averted the danger.

It was raining now. The wind was from the north-east and strengthening, and when our anchor started to drag again the decision was made to pull out and use the wind to sail south for the Barra Isles. Said Graham: 'It's going to be rough getting round the Monachs, but once the sails are up in the open sea it should be better.' At this, Dave produced some sea-sickness pills, took two and offered me two. Nor did I shun Graham's advice to go below and take his bunk in the stern for the crossing.

It was so wild that I was all but thrown out of bed. The skipper and mates had wisely decided to wear safety lines on deck. Steering the boat in these rough seas with a following wind is tricky through the white-capped grey-beards, but very thrilling with a banshee wind off the wind-whipped rigging. It took six hours to cover the 41 nautical miles and reach the calmer waters of Vatersay Sound. Two hours out of Monach we sailed from blackness into sunshine, and when I came on deck Iain reported what I had missed – a pomarine skua following kittiwakes and fulmars, harrying them to disgorge food.

163

'Where the cliff plunged to the bursting waves, above us soared the great rock wall crowned by an overhanging arch.'

Safely anchored, I was ready for supper, cooked by master mariner and chef Graham. It was squid, the first time I had tasted it, with rice, and a lovely stew to follow, plus a dram of good whisky – perfect preparation for a calm night and a sunny awakening with the wind still from the north-east. Sails up and we were away, but not to Mingulay and Barra Head as Iain had hoped, where the seas were too rough for landing, but to Pabbay, an island where I had never set foot.

Eight years ago, Graham had enthused to me about its wonderful pink rock and huge arch of overhang which he thought must be the biggest in Scotland. He had taken me as close to it as he could get in an uncomfortable swell and I had been glad when he turned away. Now, in perfect conditions, I was to have the pleasure of landing on the steeply tilted curve of white sands, in Gaelic the Bagh Ban, above which are the ruins of the former settlement.

The ruins could wait for the time being. We were anxious to climb to the top of the Hoe and descend the cliff-face to the big overhang. The climb over slabs of Lewisian gneiss bearing dwarf willow catkins yellow with pollen was delightful. We had passed the first top on the ridge and

Bagh Ban in Gaelic means 'white sands', a perfect description of the landing place on Pabbay of the Barra Isles. Its last seven islanders left when a boat failed to return from a fishing trip, it is said. Its peak population was 26 in 1881.

were descending for the next when we heard the barking of angry ravens. They were mobbing an eagle which looked huge, and as it banked steeply to evade them, we saw a second one. Undoubtedly this was a pair. We had minutes of exciting viewing before they disappeared over the horizon.

From the rocky top of the Hoe at 560 ft. we could see the houses of Castlebay and Mingulay, and Barra Head lighthouse – now fully automatic. Across the Sea of the Hebrides were Rum and Eigg, with the unmistakable outlines of the Cuillin of Skye to the north-east. In the strong breeze we felt cold, but on the slabs below the summit out of the wind we were roasted.

Graham led us down and across the rock in the direction where he thought the big overhang lay, and traversing a ledge on the face we came to the point where the cliff plunged to the bursting waves below, and above us soared the great rock wall crowned by an overhanging arch. We marvelled at its mathematical perfection, its smoothness, too blank of ledges for seabirds. It was a place to savour, all the better for its remoteness and difficulty of access.

Nor was there any easy way out. We had to go back as we came in in

165

order to cross back to the village settlement. In 1794 it supported three farming families with a peak population of 26 in 1881, falling to seven in 1911. I was told that the last families gave up and left when a boat failed to return from a fishing trip, although I am not sure if this is true.

Pabbay means Priest Island, and above the roofless ruin of a Victorian house and an older settlement is a steep mound which looks man-made, with unusual stones bearing incised crosses. Perhaps it was a chapel.

Another day we landed on what would have been a desert island, but for the tall lighthouse of Hyskeir, which has been described as ten acres of grass and much more of rock at low tide. After anchoring for the night in the snug harbour of Canna we decided to pay it a visit. Graham commented, 'It looks nothing, but wait till you get there. The light-keepers have made their own wee golf course, they grow marvellous vegetables and they fish for lobsters. I can't think of a better place for flowers or bird-life.'

Concrete paths led us half a mile to the fog-horns. We came across keeper David Noble wheelbarrowing along a pair of lobster pots. I'd met him before. I'd also met Bill Crocket, another of the lightkeepers, on Ben Vorlich when he was in the RAF Mountain Rescue team. Both men are interested in wildlife and we talked about the remarkable geology of the island whose foundation is volcanic hexagons which have been worn away and smoothed by the sea, but still retain their six-sided shape.

These men are never bored. The days simply are not long enough in summer, with lighthouse duties, gardening, golf, fishing and birdwatching. I asked about the vegetables they grow. 'Marvellous, carrots the size of your leg. Onions that keep from one year to the next, lovely potatoes, but brassicas don't do so well in the sandy soil.' I was surprised to hear that turnstones hang around the lighthouse for food in winter. The keepers also observe the passing migrants, stopping to feed between the far north nesting grounds and Europe and Africa.

The keepers do one month on this rock station and one month off, travelling by helicopter between their homes in Oban and the island. Unfortunately, it is only a matter of time before this station goes automatic and they think that within five years the only folk to come will be maintenance men and people off yachts and fishing boats.

From the top of the lighthouse we saw clearly why they will be sorry to go, for it has mighty views of the near islands of Rum, Eigg, the Cuillin of Skye, and mainland to Ardnamurchan Point and beyond.

The lighthouse, built by D. A. Stevenson in 1902, moved towards automation last April with the installation of an electric winding mechanism to turn the two and a half-ton prism-housing. Until then it had been the strong arm of the keeper on duty which did the work, 120 turns every half hour, a cold job in the winter. Now the keepers can stay below as long as the light keeps revolving. In their opinion every station will be fully automatic within the next ten years, which saddens me as well as them.

Our two final stages of this trip were to the Sound of Gunna on a favourable wind giving marvellous sailing before heading for home past the Treshnish Isles with the mountains of Mull rising in strong detail beyond, and behind us Tiree, Coll, Canna, Rum, a bit of Skye and Ardnamurchan Point. We felt we were sailing on an inland sea after our days on the open Atlantic. In the Sound of Iona the car ferry was arriving and a loaded tourist boat for Staffa leaving as we passed with a wave to the cheerful island-hoppers.

Then we passed the pink rocks of the Ross of Mull and Erraid with a lonely coast of volcanic cliffs and waterfalls mile after mile. Oban felt close when we saw the twin peaks of Ben Cruachan and the snow patches of Ben Nevis. At 4 p.m. we were turning into the yachting slip to unload our gear, pick up the car and take the road home by Loch Awe to Loch Lomond.

How lush the countryside seemed! Flowers by the wayside, the birches brilliant, the whins yellow, rhododendrons in purple bloom, and all the peaks sharp in the fine visibility. At 10 p.m. I was looking out from the window of the house to Ben Lomond where fireworks were banging and great splinters of light were making fountains of green and orange against the bulk of the mountain. It was not to celebrate my home-coming, but to mark 21 years of camping in Gartocharn by the Girl Guides.

It was certainly nice to be home, but it had been great to be away seeing new places and facing adventure. That, after all, is the spice of life.

HEBRIDEAN SEAS AND GREENLAND WATERS

IT WAS NOT until I came back from cruising in West Greenland waters and was home that I learned more about the fate of the *Laurentic* in letters responding to my appeal for information.

The *Laurentic* was a White Star liner sunk by a mine off Loch Swilly, Northern Ireland, on its way from Liverpool to Halifax. Converted to an armed merchant cruiser, she was carrying £5 million in gold bars to pay for munitions and other war materials produced in Canada and America. Disaster struck off Malin Head when she entered a minefield laid by the German submarine U.80. She sank quickly and only 121 of the 475 on board were saved.

W. A. McNeill was the chief executive officer on the ill-fated ship, and one of my correspondents, Mr Cook, wrote: 'I understand that there is a superstition amongst sailors that if they drown, their bodies drift towards home. It would be of interest to know if Lieut. (R.N.R.) McNeill was related to the MacNeils of Barra.'

Thanks to Mr Bill Petrie of Elgin, I can tell Mr Cook that when fishermen found the body on the Monachs and read the identity disc giving his name, they are reported to have said 'It's a MacNeil come home'. The island Ceann Iar, it appears, was a traditional home of this clan. Sadly, Pat McNeill, a brother of the drowned man died on active service in Flanders that same week in 1917.

Of the McNeill family, Mr Petrie writes: 'I come from the parish of Holm (Orkney) and remember the McNeills. I was no doubt delivered and baptised by the Rev. Daniel McNeill, M.D., who was minister and physician at Holm, south of Kirkwall. On the War Memorial in Holm are the names of William and Pat McNeill, two of his sons.'

With this interesting letter was appended a cutting from *The Orcadian* under a banner headline 'The Intriguing McNeill Family From Holm'. It gives a fairly detailed account of what was described as an amazing family whose best-known member was F. Marian McNeill, author of *The Scots Kitchen*, *The Silver Bough*, *Iona*, and other writings.

Their father was a Gaelic speaker from Campbeltown, and his original intention was to be a medical missionary when he graduated from Glasgow University in Arts, Divinity and Medicine. However, he was called to Holm United Free Church, married Jessie Dewar and stayed there, raising a family of 13 children, 12 of whom, six boys and six girls, survived to adulthood. Two of them graduated in Medicine and four in Arts. A centenary celebration of the birth of F. Marian McNeill was held as part of the Orkney Folk Festival last May. Duncan, youngest of the family, was author of *The Scottish Realm* and also wrote a book on that great Scot, George Buchanan.

Alan Jones of Sunderland supplied details of what happened to the *Laurentic*'s gold. He told how, lying in 120 feet of water, it became the centre of a long and dangerous salvage operation headed by Commander Damant. By 1924, the total amount of gold recovered was well over £4,000,000 at a cost of only £128,000.

For their work, Commander Damant was promoted to Captain and 11 of the divers were awarded the OBE. The salvors received half a crown for every £100 worth of gold recovered, sharing £7,000 between them.

Only 25 bars of the gold were left at the bottom of the sea and of these, three were recovered later by private enterprise.

Liverpool readers might like to know that a six-inch gun brought up from the *Laurentic* is on display in Merseyside Maritime Museum. For this information I have to thank Anthony Unwin from Cheshire who adds, 'just six years before she was sunk, the *Laurentic* did the round trip, Liverpool to Montreal and back, in 13 days and four hours, a record for the Canadian trade.'

When I read that the *Laurentic* displaced 15,000 tons I thought of the *Astor* which had taken me to Greenland. She is 19,000 tons, not very different in size. Our ship carried about 400 passengers, and one of the most popular figures was the Rev. James Currie, now of the parish of Dunlop, but an Arran man by birth, hailing from Blackwaterfoot and the family farm of Drumadoon. In fact, he was studying at Glasgow University when I worked in the neighbouring farm of Tighanfraoch, but we didn't meet till after the war, and the cruise was an excellent chance to get to know him, his wife Peggy and two of his granddaughters.

169

The Belfast-built liner Laurentic, *mined off Northern Ireland in 1917. The body of one of her crew washed ashore on the Outer Hebrides.* (The Mitchell Library, Glasgow)

He told me that he might well have become a farmer rather than a minister: 'I intended to go into agriculture even when I was in the fifth year at Keil School in Dumbarton. Then one night I had a long talk with James Mason, the headmaster. At the end of it I had changed my mind. I suppose that's what is meant by being "called".

'The three years at University were the most miserable of my life. I had to work so hard at the farm because of the war, and apart from rugby there was no time for recreation. It was all so impersonal and lonely. But my three years at Trinity College in Glasgow with kindred spirits were among my happiest days. I made good friends there and many of them came to help on the farm. Once we had 21 university degrees among the team, bunching corn!'

Captain of Keil School before leaving, and President of Trinity College, he got his M.A. in 1941 and B.D. in 1944.

How had he found the reality of the job, and how does he find it now? 'It's hard, time-consuming work dealing with people's problems. I've always put the parish first. Sunday with two services is my quietest day. It's a myth that parsons work only one day a week. At Pollok, my second charge, apart from 300 christenings and 200 weddings and a big number of funerals, I wrote at least 1,000 references and signed 750 passports a year.

'Every spare moment I had, I spent on Arran, working the farm. When

170

I took over the lease in 1959 it was a rented place and I bought it outright. I inherited eight head of cattle and built up the stock to over 120. I paid a manager, and all money made was put back into fencing, machinery and building.

'I was the fourth James Currie in a row at Drumadoon and my grandson is the sixth. My son has the farm now, but I'm still a farmer – I keep cattle at Dunlop.'

We got on to the subject of the calls made on his time at the Burns Supper season, when he can be out every night for two months.

'The first one I ever did was in 1945. I'd never been at a Burns Supper before. I gave the "Immortal Memory" and the folk liked it. I never set out to be a Burns man. Now I'm asked to do about 200 every year. Next year is booked solid. 1987 is partly booked, and I've even got one or two for 1988! I've been to Caledonian Societies in Copenhagen, Lagos, Winnipeg, Edmonton, Chicago, Dubai, and many English cities.

'There's been a radical change in attitudes towards Burns. Suppers used to be booze-ups. Now the poetry is more important. Dozens can recite the whole of "Tam o' Shanter" whereas there used to be only a few. People have been critical of me because I use humour to make people listen, but it's all related to my speech. It's not just a string of stories and a wee bit of Burns thrown in.'

He has recently returned from his 44th trip to the Holy Land. His first was in 1958, and reports of his leadership were so good that he has been taking parties averaging 60 ever since, spending one week in Jerusalem and a week in Tiberias. 'We're out every day, it's sheer happiness. I feel better known there than in Glasgow. They call us "the group that sings".'

On the cruise ship, I went to one of his Holy Land lectures, and found myself joining in the singing of 'I'm marching to Zion, beautiful, beautiful Zion' and other spritely hymns as his slides moved from one place of pilgrimage to another at fast pace, the Bible story going along cheerily and expertly. There is nothing dull about the way Currie puts it over. No wonder he can fill the kirks wherever he preaches.

Another talk he gave on the Oberammergau Passion Play was even more enthralling, and the pictures better, since they were professionally taken and held tightly to the story of the last week in the life of Jesus, with over a thousand amateur actors from the village unfolding the story from Palm Sunday to the Resurrection.

James really made the story live as he told it simply. 'It was so realistic on the stage,' he said, 'that I overheard a voice saying, as Jesus was being nailed to the cross, "Are they going to kill him?".' Last year, during the

James Currie, a minister of the Church of Scotland, who became an international celebrity through his appearances at Burns' Suppers. Toasting the National Bard Robert Burns took him to Caledonian Societies in Copenhagen, Lagos, Winnipeg, Edmonton, Chicago, Dubai, and many English cities.

ten-week period when the villagers stage the performance, James led three separate groups to see it, and I have little doubt that he will be at more performances in 1990 when it will be staged again from the beginning of June.

I was astonished with his photographic coverage of India obtained on a two-week visit when he led a church party, all the way from the Ganges plains to the Himalaya. His pictures captured the feeling of the country, the diversity of its people, the delicacy of classical architecture and scenery. In a dimly-lit factory, he showed us eight people doing needlework jobs that would be done by one person and a machine in this country.

He feels that we in this country must think along similar lines before the scourge of mass unemployment is finally resolved.

James's wife Peggy is from Tiree and was a landgirl at Drumadoon when they married in 1947. He said, 'I was told she would never make a minister's wife – too unconventional. On the farm she was a marvellous worker and could run like a hare. She cares about people, and teaches the partially-sighted in Kelvin School, Glasgow. She has been doing it for 15 years. She trained at Jordanhill after working with the mentally handicapped.'

Burly, cheerful, the humorous eyes flashing under bushy brows, James Currie is known to thousands from his 'Late Call' programmes on Scottish Television. He wouldn't deny that he likes to hold the stage and be noticed in any company, yet he told me he has always had to fight shyness. To conquer it meant being outgoing. He has certainly proved he is good at anything he takes up, including raising money for charity for which he has an impressive record.

The outbreak of war killed his chance for playing rugby for Scotland when he had been ear-marked for it. The game still means a lot, but he is saddened at the win-at-any-cost attitude which has developed. As for football, the sporting world knows of his allegiance to Rangers which has been there since he could crawl. He spoke to me with pride of being given the honour of presenting the awards given by the Scottish Professional Football Players' Association this year. 'They were fine young lads,' he said. On the topic of modern crowd behaviour, he shakes his head sadly.

Pressure of work has brought on one heart attack. I asked if he shouldn't be cutting down his workload or retiring. He only smiled.

Sadly I have to report that since this article was written James Currie died of a heart attack in 1987. He had been ploughing on the farm on Good Friday and died in the early hours of Easter Saturday. He was 66, and his borrowed time had run out.

GLEN LYON IN ALL SEASONS

THERE IS A state of tiredness when, after being out all the daylight hours among the hills, you get into your sleeping bag and every bone and muscle is comfortable on the ground and the tent-floor a perfect mattress. So it was with me, for I had been up that morning at half-past three watching blackcock on the lek, strolling about listening to the dawn chorus starting up, then among Caledonian pines to spy on velvet-antlered red deer stags before setting off for the 3,000 ft. tops to look for a rare little plover, the dotterel.

All this in Glen Lyon, at its most superb in the brilliance of newly leafing oak and ash, with primroses still blooming in the shady places and bluebells scenting the air. Camped by a burn in a secret place below the blackcock lek, it was no hardship getting out of the warm sleeping bag, for there had been no darkness, only wisps of mist settling in the hollows in the moonlight.

The first sounds to break the silence as I left the tent were from oystercatchers, a few single pipes at first, then a shrilling chorus. Next a wheatear jangled a snatch of song, and as I reached the edge of the blackcock lek two grey hens rose from my feet, females come to watch the display of the master cocks, no doubt.

In the dimness of dawn, when all you can see are white blobs dancing to an accompaniment of cat-like wails and vibrating bubbling sounds, punctuated by explosive hissings, shapes are indistinct until the light strengthens, then you can see that the white blobs are made up of a fan of grotesquely-held tail feathers, with black wings projecting from the body like paddles. Necks are blown out, and the movements are due to the birds facing up to each other and dancing back and fore, whimpering and bubbling as they advance, retire or clash head-to-head.

It was all there that morning on the flat shelf before me. Scientific

The River Lyon above Meggernie Castle flows briskly between remnant Caledonian pines.

study of blackcock has proved that the lek is a way of showing which cocks
are most dominant, and that all the grey hens will be mated by a few
dominant cocks. I have seen as many as 80 blackcock in this single area of
hillside, sub-divided into several leks. That morning I saw only eight
cocks and two grey hens. Numbers are significantly down.

I didn't stay too long at the display as I did not want to miss the dawn
chorus of the woodland birds on each side of the river at Bridge of Balgie.
They were just starting up at 4 a.m., robin first, followed by the jangle of a
redstart, trilling of wrens, shouting phrase of mistle thrush, the weary
double note of reed bunting, a whooping of peewits, then everything
became jumbled in the torrent of songs from willow warblers, song
thrushes, blackbirds, cuckoos, swallows, yaffling of green woodpecker,
discordant 'haar-haar' of crows and coo-rooing of wood pigeons.

Climbing to higher ground as the songs lessened I was among sheep
with their lambs in family groups of 15 or 20. I sat to watch colours
flooding into the world about me from the east and tingeing the high
snow-patches with pink. Time for me to go back to the tent, have a
snooze before breakfast, then go off with my wife, Rhona, to the hill.

The sun was so hot now that I was vaguely regretful at not having
begun climbing at dawn, a feeling dispelled at 2,000 ft. in a cooling breeze

175

that put life into our steps as we came into the realm of golden plover and ptarmigan near the top of Carn Gorm (3,370 ft.). Fine, high-level walking leads from here to Cairn Mairg and views are wide to Glencoe and from Loch Rannoch to Ben Alder, then eastward to the high snow-wreaths of the Cairngorms which may linger long past midsummer.

We found no dotterel, but it was a pleasure to see flowers of purple saxifrage patching the moss, and to look down on a herd of a hundred deer sunning themselves on an airy ridge. Views of river and glen as we descended confirmed my view that no other corner of the Central Highlands is so enchantingly rich in variety. Nor do I know any hills with so many ruins of summer shielings on high flanks of both sides of the glen.

A Glen Lyon man who saw the changes and wrote about them was Alexander Stewart, the scholar-shoemaker of Woodend Cottage, who died in 1941 aged 89. I did not know of him the first time I walked the glen, or of his book *A Highland Parish*, long out of print, and a classic which deserves to be reprinted with photographs bringing its history up to date.

Luckily for me, I got to know Alexandria, his daughter, who filled the gap, since she remembers when her father's house was a meeting place for the many worthies in the glen, a time of work in plenty for a whole range of local craftsmen, tailor, weaver, blacksmith, flour-miller, stone-masons, carpenters, drystane dykers, and a demand for girls as servants and boys for the farms.

She was living in the nearby village of Fortingall when I got to know her, and together we went to Woodend where her father's rusting shoe-maker's last had been laid against an outside wall. Her belief, strongly expressed, was that the years before the 1914–18 war were the happiest ones in the glen, though the pleasure had gone out of shoe-making for her father because, by 1900, ready-made footwear was cheaper and readily available, and the craftsman's trade had been reduced to unprofitable repairs. So he gave it up, and became a salesman for an Edinburgh publishing firm selling historical books.

Seton Gordon, whose writings are full of historical titbits gathered from personal contacts with all classes of Highlanders tells of the pleasure of meeting the old shoe-maker and being taken by him on a conducted tour in 1938. He told Gordon that when he was young the population of the glen had been 700, but at the time of their walk it was down to 200. At the time of writing in 1990 it is less than half that number, and the Primary School roll is 14.

It was following the defeat of the Jacobites at Culloden that the clan system was broken, sheep were introduced on a big scale, forests were destroyed, and mass emigration encouraged in the 19th century, and in Alexander Stewart's time the economy of Glen Lyon was in sheep farming and sport, which caused him to write:

> O shame that the native mountaineer
> Must give way to the grouse and
>   antlered deer.
>
> On his native heath he had prior claim,
> To the southern sportsman in
>   search of game.

His daughter Alexandria, who wrote a little book, *The Glen That Was*, became a school teacher, and taught for a time in a house so far west in this longest glen in Scotland that she got home only for weekends, by horse-drawn trap. Her school was a shepherd's house, and her class his young family. The lonely dwelling was on the edge of Loch Lyon, a two-mile stretch of water with a shepherding family at each end. I spoke to one of the shepherds in the mid-1930s, the only time I ever walked right through the glen from Bridge of Orchy to Loch Tayside. I remember him telling me that the two families got their provisions every six months.

What Alexandria remembers is how lively the glen was with so many young folk providing their own entertainment, cards, draughts, singing and dancing to the strains of the melodian, or forming rinks when the ice was thick enough in winter for curling competitions. In spring the horses were ornamentally decked up for ploughing matches held in the fields of Glen Lyon House.

The father could never have envisaged the changes his daughter was to see in the post-Hitler-War years, as a dam 1,700 ft. long doubled the length of Loch Lyon and raised its level from 100 ft. to 170 ft., inundating the shepherds' cottages. Two other lochs, Loch Daimh and Loch Giorra became one and the farm between them was submerged when a 1,500 ft. concrete dam was built. From this reservoir, noted for its trout fishing, water rushes along 3½ miles of tunnel and 1,680 ft. of pipe-line south to Cashlie Power Station just two miles from the big dam in Glen Lyon. A headpond at Stronuich provides compensation for the river. Local opinion is that control of the River Lyon has had an adverse effect on the salmon fishing.

Nevertheless, the salmon still leap just south of Bridge of Balgie where

177

the Lyon runs rough and the fish send up arrowheads of spray as they flail through the rapids, mounting upwards with zig-zag body movements. Taking a photograph, one seemed to fill the viewfinder as I snapped. At the same moment I felt a thud and something brush my left leg. It was a fat kipper-coloured salmon, its elongated snout was actually bumping my boot as, wriggling and threshing, it turned its body and plopped back into the waterfall, to be swept down; and no doubt it would try again and maybe get its aim right next time.

That October morning, when the salmon took the wrong slant, had started for us with a rush of fieldfares and redwings, so many landing at once on the rowan berries that branches were breaking off. Gutteral 'chacks' mingled with squeaks and yelps as wave after wave passed east down the glen, perhaps having crossed Rannoch Moor, using the deep trench of the glen as a flyway.

Overjoyed to see our first Scandinavian migrants of the season, our spirits were further raised by the pale disc of the sun, and soft Persian-rug colours beginning to brighten; orange bracken contrasting with tawny deer grass, and silver-barked birches shining with gold leaves. To do justice to the rioting colours of oaks, chestnuts, beeches and aspens would have needed the brush of Picasso. At a stop we had siskins and redpolls and a party of 30 long-tailed tits dancing above our heads in a ripple of churring notes.

Delightful Bridge of Balgie spans the River Lyon and, crossing it, a narrow single-track road that has to be driven with care twists and turns in a climb to 1,600 ft. before descending to Loch Tayside. The hamlet at Bridge of Balgie is Glen Lyon's centre of commerce, with shop, houses and primary school. And just beyond the bridge is the Gatehouse and driveway to Meggernie Castle, the mansion house of the estate, strictly private of course.

The driving road westward climbs above Meggernie, a white castle on green flats backed by an open forest of Caledonian pines, where the river twists through rocky rapids. It always worried me that these priceless remnants of primeval woodland were being allowed to decay, while much of the mid-glen was being smothered in commercial spruces. Until the 1980s the attitude of the sporting estate owner was 'The ancient trees give good shelter in winter to the deer. Where would they go if we fenced the pines to keep them out?'

But when higher cash grants were made in conjunction with good management a large part of Glen Lyon's Caledonian wood above Meggernie Castle was fenced, and the remainder left open to shelter the deer in winter. Seedling pines and some broad-leaved trees that were planted are growing well. Nor is that all. Grants have been made to glen farmers to fence their small woodlands and allow natural regeneration. In addition, the farmers have been encouraged by grants to use organic fertilisers on their grazings and arable fields for the benefit of insects and birds.

Alexandria Stewart's little book *The Glen That Was* records much of worth that hasn't changed in scenic terms. Alas, however, many of the tradition bearers that I knew in my own time have vanished. One was the cheerful little lady who kept the village shop, Miss Hattie Macdonald. Always when my wife and I called we were whisked into her back-shop parlour, and before she moved to the teapot we would say, 'Now don't bother to make tea', well knowing that her reply would be 'It's not the bother, but the expense', her stout little body shaking with laughter as she got on with the preparation.

Nothing happened in the glen without her knowing it, and she was a great favourite with the late Meggernie Castle owner, Sir Edward Wills. Tramps using the glen as a through-route to the west could depend on a hand-out and the use of a shed to doss in. Glen Lyon was such a home-from-home to us that we even considered selling our Loch Lomond house and buying one that was for sale in a favoured spot above the river. But looking back now with hindsight, I think we would have found the glen a sad place with all our old friends gone.

However, the glen itself still retains its magic. The twisting roads leading into it are still single-track and require great care. Upgrading these roads would be a mistake in my view, for this is not a glen to whisk through, but one to explore for its peace and beauty. As yet tourism does not rule in Glen Lyon.

BEHOLD, THE HEBRIDES!

IN A LIFETIME devoted to the hills I've just spent one of the most unusual days of my life, beginning in Tarbert, Harris, where I climbed into a helicopter bound for South Uist. And given 365 days in the year to choose from, the morning could hardly have been better: superb visibility after rain; warm sun and not too much wind for comfortable flying. Even my keenest anticipations were exceeded as the whirring blades spun faster and faster. The moment of fast vertical lift-off is always exciting, more so today because in seconds I found myself shouting, 'Look! St Kilda!' No mistaking the blue humps and rock stacks a good 40 miles out in the ocean.

At the same time I was trying to register a unique view of Tarbert below me, a neck of grey rock separating the piers of the West Loch and East Loch. But for that neck, South Harris would be an island and our flight line showed us its amazing scenic contrasts. On the western side, the great horseshoe sweeps of Luskentyre sands backed by emerald green croftlands. To the east, an ice-scalped rock desert of Lewisian gneiss speckled with peaty lochans cut up by inlets of the sea where white crofts perched beside tiny patches of cultivation. Having stayed there, I know the attraction of this Bays district whose winding east road leads to Rodel.

We came over the very point where west and east roads meet at Loch Rodel pier, and while I was craning my neck to enjoy the unusual view of its famous Church of St Clements, I could hear our pilot, John Poland, talking on the radio to Benbecula Airport, and being asked to keep his weather eye open for a small aeroplane which had gone missing over the Uists.

The island-studded Sound of Harris stretched ahead, and after so many sailing trips through it in recent years I could take in at a glance its tricky navigation problems stretching to populous Berneray which is so

Tarbert, Harris, a town on a neck of land that separates the East Loch from the West Loch. But for that neck, South Harris would be an island.

good for crofting and lobstering. I could see the fields and houses dotted along its four miles of narrow road, and the lovely freshwater loch behind the hills. I remembered how proud of their island the happy folk were as they told me how their cattle beasts invariably fetch the best prices going at the Lochmaddy sales.

The distance to that market as the helicopter flies is only eight miles, but what a fantastic jigsaw of land and water North Uist is on its grim eastern side! Once, after floundering among bogs and being cut off by lochs, I had given up the attempt to climb the North and South Lee from Lochmaddy. Looking down I could appreciate why. To climb the highest peak, Eaval (1,138 ft.), I had sailed in to the head of Loch Eport with Graham Tiso, then set off along freshwater Loch Obisary which almost encircles the peak dominating a land of water.

The causeways spanning the North Ford and South Ford have taken away the tidal problems and dangers which used to beset travellers journeying to Benbecula and South Uist whose populations, like those of North Uist, are mainly on the sandy Atlantic side, delightfully visible this morning as we edged westward over Loch Druidibeg, breeding strong-hold of greylag geese and red-necked phalaropes.

181

Milton, Flora MacDonald's birthplace, was as far south as we flew for reasons of fuel. Now we swung east for Beinn Mhor to swoop over its ridge and down over the big cliffs of Coire Hellisdale which has a little perched lochan discharging into Coradale Bay facing the Cuillin of Skye, and Rum. This is where Bonnie Prince Charlie spent his happiest three weeks in the five months after Culloden when he was on the run.

But he didn't live in the cave shown as his refuge on the Ordnance Survey map. There was better accommodation in a good bothy much visited by the Clanranald MacDonalds who fitted him out with a tartan suit and supplied enough wine and brandy for a mammoth carousal lasting three days, when Charlie drank them all under the table, including Boisdale who had a great reputation for the bottle.

Charlie amused himself on the hills, shooting birds and red deer for the pot and seeing a French ship in every sail on the horizon. His peaceful period ended when hundreds of troops were landed to comb the island from the north and south until they met in the middle. Only the presence of a 'fifth column' within the searching enemy troops enabled the fugitives to keep one step ahead.

His escape to Skye dressed as Flora MacDonald's Irish maid, Betty Burke, was made from Rossinish in Benbecula just north up the coast where we flew next, a ragged headland as empty today as in Charlie's time.

With my head still full of these long ago events I felt a little like a time-traveller when we touched down on the school playing-field in Tarbert at lunch-time. For the last touch of Jacobite realism, we had even seen a tall ship with its sails spread, beating across our bows. It was the *Eye of the Wind*, bigger by far than any of the small ships of the British and French navies searching for engagements in the '45.

Where now? The day was young, my companion Allan and I were still fresh, and there was Clisham, the highest hill in Harris, only five miles away. So along the Stornoway road we drove to leave the car by Loch a' Mhorghain and in quick time we were in the company of golden plovers, wheatears and meadow pipits as we made good time up its grassy flank to the steepening ridge.

I had climbed this highest peak in the Outer Hebrides, 2,622 ft., only once before, 30 years ago. Then, bad weather from the Atlantic had engulfed us. For a time it looked as if I was going to be unlucky again as a general greyness dimmed the distance and obscured the sun. However, it didn't develop to rain until we were down, so we had the fulfilment of views all the way, in the east, to Loch Shell and the Shiant Islands of happy camping memories and boulderfield days among the whirring puffins, razorbills and guillemots. These islands are formed of the most northerly columnar basalt in Britain, the youngest rocks on the very edge of the oldest, the Lewisian gneiss.

And we got a good scramble on the old rocks by detouring a bit before joining the narrow summit ridge lifting nobly to a fine pointed top. Now we could look on the lumpy chain of peaks stretching west to Hushinish sands at the very end of the west road where I had camped on my first trip to Harris when I felt I had reached the very edge of the world.

At that time the sail from Mallaig on touring ships took not only a day but a night as well. Perhaps that was why they were so well-appointed, like mini-liners, even to the extent of a waiter service of beautifully served meals on well-laid tables each with a sparkling white linen cloth.

That long dream-like sail still feels as if it happened recently, passing the blue islands of Eigg and Rum, then the lavender greys of the Cuillin ridge, every loved serration sharply incised, the Inaccessible Pinnacle, the notch of the Thearlaich-Dubh gap, Sgurr Mhic Coinnich and Alasdair, from whose summits we had first looked with longing on Harris of the Big Hills. Now we were going there.

That's what travel is about, anticipation before realisation. Lochboisdale was our first contact with the Outer Islands, astir with activity, for we had caught the evening tail-end of a cattle sale, with two of MacBrayne's cargo boats tied up and the air loud with Gaelic cries as beasts were penned for shipment. Even the bales of hay and boxes of Glasgow bread were directed out of the hold by Gaelic voices.

The sun was setting by the time we left, its rose light lingering on the bare grey gneiss above a glass-calm sea reflecting a sky of palest blue. Yes – enchanted islands, but it was 9.30 in the morning before we got to Tarbert. The shops were closed and we stopped a postman to ask when they opened. 'This is the middle of the night in Harris,' he laughed. 'You'll get nothing here before 11 o'clock.' He was right.

We were luckier than we knew, however, for we had arrived on the right day for the bus to Hushinish and we squeezed aboard that afternoon. Squeezed is the correct word, for it contained everything except passengers – a full-sized bath, a water-closet with pipes, yes and a kitchen sink, not to mention tins of petrol and paraffin drums, bits of furniture, loaves of bread and boxes of food. As for the road, it was like a rough mountain track, plunging steeply up and down, past lonely houses and tiny squares of oats and potatoes, the smallest fields we had ever seen, carved from the peat.

183

Bringing home the peats from the moor on Harris.

What makes this distant trip so vivid in my mind now? Because in Tarbert, on the very next morning after the helicopter flight, a stockily built man clapped me on the shoulder and grasped my hand in an iron grip. 'You're back again. You mind I took you to Hushinish in my bus.' Talking to him about times so very different from today brought it all back, especially a meeting with the peat-cutters of the island of Scarp under the slopes of Huseval Mor.

We'd been climbing and birding that day, seeing arctic skuas chasing terns, finding nests of oystercatchers and ring plovers, watching red-throated divers flying in from the sea to their nesting lochans, enjoying the sight of basking sharks and Atlantic seals and were heading back to the tent well-pleased when we came on the peat gatherers, mothers, fathers, children busily bagging the winter fuel to boat it across to an island whose houses we could see just across the water. Work stopped as we approached and we were waved to a fire where a big teapot was steaming and soon they were filling us out a cup and yarning cheerily.

'There's nobody on Scarp now, not a soul,' said the bus driver. 'They all left. Young folk have no use for the hard ways of crofting.' Not, we agreed, that this is surprising in a world where everybody expects the modern standard of living which you do not get at subsistence level without a weekly wage packet.

Spinning the wool from the sheep to make the famous Harris tweed, a cottage industry of the Outer Hebrides.

In the Hebrides generally the only viable islands are those where cash can be earned. Scalpay at the mouth of East Loch Tarbert is a case in point. At the time when Bonnie Prince Charlie landed on it in 1746 there was only one family. Today its population is around 450 and it is a real hive of activity because of fishing, as I saw when I visited it this year.

My first visit to Scalpay was five years ago and I had been immediately impressed by its vitality. The harbour scene in 1981 was very much as I remembered it, fishermen busy on their boats painting, repairing, doing engineering jobs, preparing nets, all to make ready for an early morning departure for the fishing grounds on Monday morning.

Just to be there made you feel good. It had the feeling of a place that is cared for and good to live in; modern houses with flower gardens, milk cows grazing, wee fields growing strips of oats and potatoes on the crofts, and Gaelic the universal language. Fish were scarce, they were telling me, and the price for prawns poor, but Scalpachs have never had it easy and don't expect to.

Returning by ship to Uig on Skye I thought I'd pay a visit to the Island of Raasay by crossing from Sconser on the modern car ferry, remembering how hard the islanders fought for it to keep their island from going down beyond recall.

RETURN TO RAASAY

EVER SINCE MY first visit to Raasay in 1971, I've thought of this narrow island, lying parallel with Skye and the Applecross coast, as the true 'Green Isle of the Great Deep' – with apologies to Neil M. Gunn! Raasay, because of the depth of its good soil, truly is green. But there is an unfortunate connection with the colour, too – the Sussex pathologist Dr John Green, who acquired key properties at bargain prices from the Scottish Department of Agriculture and then let them rot. He also frustrated a plan for a car ferry terminal at a landing place below the listed mansion, Raasay House, which he said would become a first class hotel. After some renovations had been carried out on the house, he abandoned it to wind and weather.

I heard the story of this extraordinary small-time capitalist from Alexander Nicolson, chief spokesman against Dr Green, when we stayed with him in 1971 in Churchtown House, known locally as the 'Tailor's House', the tailor being the father of the Gaelic poet, Dr Sorley Maclean, whose connection with Raasay goes back beyond eight generations. His poetry reflects its tragic history, and with only a dozen young men left on the island, Nicolson, then County Councillor, boat hirer and lobster fisherman, was concerned at the apparent inability of the authorities to combat Dr Green.

Nicolson was campaigning at that time for a car ferry between Sconser in Skye and the little harbour in Clachan Bay, and also for a breakwater between two natural reefs which would have made a fishing industry possible and helped keep young men on the island. Dr Green's response was categoric and devious, considering that since his purchases he had visited the island only once. He wrote:

'Raasay is an island of outstanding natural beauty where you can get right away from modern life. In my view the whole idea of a ferry scheme is hopelessly uneconomic and perfectly stupid. If the islanders don't like conditions as they are, they can leave.'

Green was in the tradition of too many of Raasay's past owners, who, having obtained key properties were unconcerned about the welfare of the islanders. The most active Raasay folk wanted to get into the mainstream of modern life, not away from it. They saw hope of this through a car ferry which would attract tourists to make the short crossing from Skye. Also it would make it possible to go by ferry and bus to Portree and back in a day, a journey that would be a great help to crofters requiring to go to the market in Skye. The Scottish Office dilly-dallied and it took seven and a half years before action was finally taken. In 1974 a compulsory purchase order obtained the site desired for a ferry-slip, but surveys showed it would be too expensive to develop and so the terminal had to be at Suisnish.

Arriving off the car ferry this summer, I wondered what changes I would see 15 years on from my first arrival here in the wee cargo and passenger vessel *Loch Arkaig*, then sailing between Kyle and Portree. At Sconser all the signs were that the ferry trade was brisk, with a line of waiting cars far beyond its capacity and hosts of backpackers bound for the Youth Hostel and Raasay Outdoor Centre. My wife and a group of her Ladies' Scottish Climbing Club friends were heading for the Centre's self-catering quarters, while I was booked to stay on a croft at Oscaig.

Wheeling my bike ashore at Suisnish, I was wondering what those who had never been to Raasay before would think of the skyline of dereliction with dismal hunks of concrete and the grey remains of old storage sheds.

The pier beside the car-ferry terminal was built to take away iron ore, mined from underground shafts inland, brought out in bogies and conveyed to the pier area by an overhead transport system. These ruins date to the First World War when the miners were mostly German prisoners, together with some locals. The low grade ore was valuable when iron for munitions was in short supply, but in peacetime it did not pay the cost of extraction and the workings were abandoned.

New arrivals who might have been depressed by that introduction to Raasay must have felt more cheerful when, in just over a mile, they came into Churchtown Bay and the populous little village of Inverarish with its double rows of neat houses built for the miners. Up the hill, past the new hotel and the stables, a driveway leads to Raasay House where the ladies had a sitting room, a kitchen and dormitory-wing to themselves. Just a mile on from there was the modern bungalow where I was to stay with crofter Calum Don Mackay and his wife Rebecca – a happy pair whose Gaelic singing delighted the three of us who were their guests.

After a very wet start to the holiday on our first morning as we explored around the strange pinnacle of Brochel Castle, quite suddenly the skies cleared, out came the sun and we set off for the rocky north on a smooth tarmac road. The last time I was here it was just a bed of stones which had been carefully laid by one man using a barrow, pick and shovel. When I met Calum MacLeod in 1971 he had been working at the road for five years. He finished it in 1976.

I had two splendid days with the more energetic of the Climbing Club ladies. The second was particularly memorable, when we reached Eilean Tigh, accessible only at low tide and as far north as you can go on this narrowing north end of Raasay. Across a seaweedy short strait, a short rock scramble, and the way to the peaklet offered a choice of steep bands of Lewisian gneiss leading to a pointed top.

Due starboard of us was the big inlet of Loch Torridon at the head of the Applecross peninsula with Ben Alligin and Liathach emerging from waddings of white cloud. And just across the water, less than a half mile away, lay the bare edge of South Rona, which although looking impossible of settlement, had given a living to three townships of folk cleared from the more fertile lands of Raasay. In the Census of 1851 Rona held 106 folk, and even more afterwards, living mainly on fish, and carrying up seaweed in creels from the shore to make the thin soil suitable for growing potatoes.

The people of Raasay were renowned as good fishers, and in 1787 the impoverished MacLeod Chief gave details to the Government of the fine natural harbours on Rona, the abundance of fish in the waters and the low costs of providing boats and equipment. Successive landlords could have acted on this, but nothing was done. Owing to inshore trawling over the years fish are scarce and now any boats you see are trawling for prawns.

Eilean Tigh, the tidal island on which we stood is a lovely spot. The Gaelic word *tigh* means house, and its ruins are in the bracken below the rocks. Made of square-cut blocks of Lewisian gneiss, it was lived in until the 1930s by Johnny Mor, big John Nicolson, whose job it was to ferry the mail between Raasay and Rona. He was the grandfather of Alexander Nicolson with whom I stayed on my first visit to Raasay, and who is now the Master of the car ferry.

188 The man I was eager to speak to was the road-builder extraordinary,

Calum MacLeod on the road he built with his own hands. It took him 10 years, and during that time he wore out two wheelbarrows, six picks, six shovels, four spades and five hammers.

Calum MacLeod, but it took me three visits to his croft at Arnish before I found him at home, as he was so busy with his sheep. At 74 years of age and after 47 years in the lighthouse service, he is a good advertisement for Raasay. He is a natural scholar and historian, though his only schooling was at Torran which he left at 14. He married the school's last teacher, whose pupils had reached the stage when they could be counted on one hand.

Talking about depopulation of the roadless north end, he told me, 'When I began on the road there were seven families at this end. When I finished it 10 years later there were only ourselves. I hope the road will bring people here to settle again. A retired couple have already done so, and I think it would be a good thing if Raasay people who have worked away from the island, and want to come back to retire, were given a small holding and the right to build a house.'

He told me about his own life: at 16, working as a deck boy on the attendance boat serving Rona lighthouse, eventually becoming its master, and then becoming a lighthouse keeper on Rona, a rock station at which he did duty for a month on and a month off. 'It makes me proud when I see vehicles now where before you couldn't take a handbarrow. I counted 20 cars going past when I was working at the sheep yesterday, and I've seen 17 in the car park.'

I drove him down to Brochel Castle and back just to hear him telling me about the 10 years he spent building the road. When we came to the first of the two cattle grids, he said, 'I was told I would have to pay £1,000 each for them, which I couldn't afford. Then one day I met two gentlemen from Kent, and happened to mention the grids. One of them was just about to take delivery of cattle grids at £100 each, and offered me two at that price. That's how I got them.'

He had gone about the surveying systematically, sending away to a secondhand bookshop for a book he had seen advertised, *Road Making and Maintenance* by Thomas Aitken. A Major Mitcham and Captain Harrison gave him some advice, and the Department of Agriculture provided explosives, a driller, blaster and compressor. In 1966 he began his 3,000-yard self-imposed task. He was convinced that it was the only way he would get a road, for in 1925, when 92 adults signed a petition asking for a cart-road to Torran, it was refused.

Surveys for a road had been done, but a route had never been pegged the way Calum took. Sheep always seek the easiest way over the hills, and by watching them and marking their routes with stones, at the same time noting the natural drainage pattern, he worked out where his culverts should be and where drystone walls would have to be built. The hardest bit was the wooded section on the climb above Brochel when he had to remove giant roots and carry rocks to make a foundation.

Although the road was improved and tarred by the authorities five years ago, Calum's work wasn't finished, for there was still a roadless section of 360 yards to his own house. He completed this stretch in 1985, and just before my visit the final coat of tar went down. The Crofters' Commission, who provided a grant of £2,000, were delighted with his work, and the final tarring was done by the Highland Regional Council.

Calum was born in Glasgow of Raasay parents, but when the war broke out in 1914 and London got its first Zeppelin raid, his father, who was at sea as a quartermaster, sent Calum and his mother to Arnish for safety. The only memento he has of his father is a silver watch, and as he showed me it he also produced a little gold medal and chain. It was awarded him by the New York Celtic Society for a Gaelic essay he wrote as a schoolboy. He has won other prizes, and he is at present writing a book on the great men of Raasay.*

In six hours of conversation with him and his wife Lexie, my wife and I were hospitably entertained and Calum showed me his vast collection of

* Calum MacLeod died in 1988.

Raasay House in its splendid setting looking out to the Isle of Skye. After being allowed to fall into decay, the house has been refurbished and is having a new lease of life as an outdoor centre providing a wide range of adventure courses.

photographs, some of people evicted from the island. He corresponds with around 28 families in Australia, New Zealand, Cape Town, the USA and Canada, descendants of people cleared from Raasay between 1851 and 1854. Since the road was built, many visitors from abroad, descended from evicted islanders, have called on him.

That was the best indoor day. All the days outside were good. One of the best was when we climbed to the top of Dun Caan by its western side, and directly down east by a gully, the crags of which seemed improbable, yet proved quite easy. It led to an oval of loch and on to the double-tiered crofting settlement of Hallaig, a place of magical charm, with birchwoods and crags above, and the seashore below rich in fossil ammonites and tiny life forms from 350 million years ago.

Another day we walked all the way down the roadless coast from Screapadale, transported to the starting point in vehicles provided by Raasay Outdoor Centre.* Beginning in woodland, there was never a dull moment in this undulating traverse, where sometimes we were forced by

* Details of courses and prices at Raasay Outdoor Centre can be obtained by writing to the Outdoor Centre, Isle of Raasay, by Kyle, Ross-shire IV40 8PB. (Tel: 047862 266.)

crags down to the shore, then up again, always with fine views out to the Applecross shore and the sharp peaks of Kintail.

Our final day was so brilliantly clear, with north-westerly winds, that five of us went to Dun Caan again for a view that extended from Ben More, Mull, to the peaks of north-west Ross and Sutherland. Eager to stay high, Rhona and I found a lovely walk to a point where we could cross the road and descend by the steep wooded glen to the beach at Inver.

What about Raasay House itself? I was impressed by it as an outdoor centre. The three young folk who run it live there all year. They rent it from the Highlands and Islands Development Board, and people who come on courses can have them tailored to suit their own requirements. The courses include elementary rock climbing, canoeing and wind-surfing, camping and bothying, ecology and Hebridean exploration in a good motor launch.

The instructors, in their spare time, have done much with paint brushes to restore the beautifully-proportioned rooms to something of their original splendour. Heating is a problem, especially in winter, and a fund is accumulating to install central heating as soon as possible.

Raasay Social Services use the west wing as a community hall, and provided a grand ceilidh on our last night with excellent pipers and singers and a marvellous young dancer. Included in the £1 admission were tea, soft drinks, sandwiches, cakes and a wee dram if you wanted it – great value and a grand memory to take away from one of the most delightful of islands.